Towards a Cultural Philology
Phèdre and the Construction of 'Racine'

THE EUROPEAN HUMANITIES RESEARCH CENTRE

UNIVERSITY OF OXFORD

The European Humanities Research Centre of the University of Oxford organizes a range of academic activities, including conferences and workshops, and publishes scholarly works under its own imprint, LEGENDA. Within Oxford, the EHRC bridges, at the research level, the main humanities faculties: Modern Languages, English, Modern History, Literae Humaniores, Music and Theology. The Centre stimulates interdisciplinary research collaboration throughout these subject areas and provides an Oxford base for advanced researchers in the humanities.

The Centre's publications programme focuses on making available the results of advanced research in medieval and modern languages and related interdisciplinary areas. An Editorial Board, whose members are drawn from across the British university system, covers the principal European languages. Titles include works on French, German, Italian, Portuguese, Russian and Spanish literature. In addition, the EHRC co-publishes with the Society for French Studies, the British Comparative Literature Association and the Modern Humanities Research Association. The Centre also publishes *Oxford German Studies* and has launched a Special Lecture Series under the LEGENDA imprint.

Enquiries about the Centre's publishing activities should be addressed to:
Professor Malcolm Bowie, Director

Further information:
Kareni Bannister, Senior Publications Officer
European Humanities Research Centre
47 Wellington Square, Oxford OX1 2JF
enquiries@ehrc.ox.ac.uk
www.ehrc.ox.ac.uk

LEGENDA

RESEARCH MONOGRAPHS IN FRENCH STUDIES

LEGENDA

EUROPEAN HUMANITIES RESEARCH CENTRE
RESEARCH MONOGRAPHS IN FRENCH STUDIES 4

Towards a Cultural Philology
Phèdre and the Construction of 'Racine'

❖

Amy Wygant

LEGENDA

European Humanities Research Centre
University of Oxford
Research Monographs in French Studies 4
1999

Frontispiece. Sir Peter Paul Rubens
The Death of Hippolytus. Cambridge: The Fitzwilliam Museum

LEGENDA

European Humanities Research Centre
Research Monographs in French Studies 4

CONTENTS

For My Parents

ACKNOWLEDGEMENTS

It is a pleasure to thank teachers, colleagues and students to whose encouragement and provocation this book owes much. In Baltimore, Wilda Anderson, Rüdiger Campe, Milad Doueihi, Pier Massimo Forni, Christopher Fox, Claire Lyu, Rainer Nägele, Richard Rand and Ron Walters talked me through its inception. In Los Angeles, the late George Bauer, Marie-Florine Bruneau and Peter Starr welcomed me and oversaw its transformation. In the UK, Noël Peacock and Michael Moriarty have generously presided over its conclusions.

For financial support, I remain grateful to the Department of French and the Charles S. Singleton Center for Italian Studies of the Johns Hopkins University; the Andrew W. Mellon Foundation and the University of Southern California Department of French and Italian; and the Faculty of Arts, the Department of French and the Grants Committee of the University of Glasgow.

ILLUSTRATIONS

Chapter 3

INTRODUCTION

❖

Racine *enraciné*

This study is devoted to achieving an understanding of Racine's *Phèdre* by pivoting the tragedy through a number of its cultural contexts. The name of Racine is synonymous with classicism; the *Oxford English Dictionary* defines 'classic' with reference to Racine. But the classicism of the Racinian text has not always impressed its readers as overwhelming or even necessary. The subject of Racine has occupied mystics, Romantics, structuralists, Marxists and musicians,[1] and the Racinian text has been declared both sublime and ridiculous.[2] Heard as now lyric, now prosaic,[3] it has served not just as the zenith of the classical aesthetic but also as the epitome of the baroque.[4] There has recently been a certain interest in biography:[5] the Jean Racine who has been considered both an apologist for political repression and an object of it,[6] and who was once identical with the documents of his professional career, led, it would seem, a chameleon's life.[7] There has been a welcome insistence upon the properly theatrical and rhetorical aspects of the tragedies,[8] and, this dimension of the Racinian stage re-emphasized, the gap between theory and practice has been reread, with the result that the famous unities are under pressure. The most important aspect of Racinian time is not its continuity, and the *palais à volonté* as the classical spirit made manifest, the ultimate expression of unity of place, is no more.[9]

Accordingly, we might well wonder what this textual object might be, and what quality or aspect of it might account for its protean availability. My argument is that Racine the energizer, a text capable at once of determining and disappearing into any number of readings, is a Racine *enraciné*. It evinces a rootedness in its own time and place which is so radical as to produce multiplicity as its own consequence. The work of a cultural philology is to bring out some of the meanings of this state of affairs.

In terms Nietzschean and Auerbachian, the expression 'cultural philology' is tautological, for each practised a philology which served an inquiry into culture. Auerbach argued with Vico that 'philology investigates what the various peoples regarded as true at each cultural stage and what accordingly formed the basis of their actions and institutions'.[10] This philology was broadly contextual and synonymous with philosophy: 'The systematic context of all human history [...] we may equally well call philology or philosophy. This philological philosophy or philosophical philology is concerned with only one thing—mankind.' The 27-year-old Nietzsche, delivering his inaugural address as Professor of Classical Philology at the University of Basel in 1869, pronounced his 'confession of faith' (*Glaubensbekenntniss*) to be 'that all philological activities should be enclosed and surrounded by a philosophical view of things, in which everything individual and isolated is evaporated as something detestable, and in which great homogenous views alone remain'.[11] In this advocacy of a globalized philology, Nietzsche and Auerbach offer particularly important formulations of one notion of philology inherited from Latin antiquity.

Its broad meaning, which in the nineteenth century became 'the love or the study of learning and literature; the investigation of a language and its literature, or of languages and literatures, for the light they cast upon men's character, activity, and history',[12] is indeed the only meaning to be found in the late seventeenth-century French dictionaries which define the term. The *Dictionnaire des Arts et des sciences* of Thomas Corneille offers 'espece de Science universelle, qui s'étend sur toute sorte de connoissances'. Similarly, the *Dictionnaire* of Furetière offers 'en un mot, une litterature universelle qui s'étend sur toutes sortes de sciences & d'Auteurs'. Furetière cites, as does the earliest usage given in English by the *OED*, the fourth-century allegory of Martianus Capella, 'The Marriage of Philology and Mercury'. 'This slender girl Philology' of Martianus 'discusses the heavens, the seas, seething Tartarus, for whole nights at a time, and traverses in her careful research the homes of all the gods; [she] considers the constitution of the world, the girding circles, the parallels, the oblique circles and colors, the poles and climates and rotations, and the multitude of the stars themselves'. Philology's handmaidens, given to her by Mercury, are the seven liberal arts.[13]

There is, then, a powerful and lengthy tradition of philology as a generalized appropriation of all that is to be known. Auerbach assigned to the early eighteenth century its turn to historicism, philology then becoming a pursuit of all that is to be known about the past, and the platform had thus been constructed for the appearance of the national philologies,[14] as well as for the equation of philology with medievalism.[15] Philology circled back to the present when scholars in nineteenth-century Germany, France and England used its powers in order to be able to assert national identities. Max Müller, the first German philologist to be appointed at Oxford, was able to imagine 'us' in terms of the inheritance which philology discovers:

> The classical scholar uses Greek or Latin, the oriental scholar Hebrew or Sanskrit, or any other language, as a key to an understanding of the literary monuments which bygone ages have bequeathed to us, as a spell to raise from the tomb of time the thoughts of great men in different ages and different countries, and as a means ultimately to trace the social, moral, intellectual, and religious progress of the human race.[16]

This philological witchcraft, philology as 'a spell', is itself a weighty inheritance.[17] It explains how Jacques Lacan can be called 'a comparative philologist in the grand Victorian manner',[18] and how the most recently formulated of historicisms can declare, 'I began with a desire to speak with the dead.'[19]

However, thinking about history has swung away from the valorization of the 'progress of the human race' and from the assumption that 'every age has its characteristic unity'.[20] There is now a thinking 'beyond *Zeitgeist*', which would emphasize historical discontinuity, separateness, multiplicity and particularity.[21] In this connection, philology offers an opportunity, for parallel to its history as the tool of a reconstructed totality is a history of its overwhelming interest in specificity. One of its meanings is equivalent to its etymology, 'love of speech or argument', which opposes it to philosophy, 'love of wisdom'. The *OED*'s examples of this meaning from the seventeenth century include 'babbling' and 'discoursive noise'. It is in this sense that Nietzsche can refer to philology as 'a kind of sham monarchy' (*Scheinmonarchie*, 146, 250) composed of 'wholly different scientific and aesthetico-ethical impulses'. The Philology of Martianus has as one of her handmaidens Periergia, whose meaning is overelaboration, the taking of excessive pains.[22] In order to ascend to immortality, Philology must necessarily rid her body of its accumulated learning, which she proceeds to do by bringing it up 'in spasms': 'That nausea and labored vomit turned into a stream of writings of all kinds' (47).

What this means for a methodology is that philology contains within itself both the fetish of the fragment, and the will fantastically to extrapolate from the particular a generality. Philology has always trodden the thin line between the spirit of the collector and the spirit of the philosopher, lending itself now to the one project, now to the other. Like the text of Racine itself, philology has proven to be radically available, and it is this quality which makes its concern with detail and its drive towards totality an appropriate logic for the studies of Racine's *Phèdre* included here. And if this philology is specified as a 'cultural philology', it is not just to produce an unexpected coupling of a critical buzz-word,[23] with an antiquarian word under whose aegis currently are to be found publishing projects as varied as 'the structure, history and relationships of languages', British literature before 1900 and 'research in medieval and modern literature',[24] and whose main recent interest has been among medievalists.[25] Rather, this coupling insists upon the reference both to the long tradition of inquiry which approaches philology to a totalized culture, and to more recent scholarship, which speaks not of culture but rather of cultures.

The first three chapters of the study which follows attempt to tread this philological line. In the first, an answer is suggested to the question: If this splendid collection of verse is not the tragedy, as Racine himself reportedly said upon completing the tragedy's prose sketch, then what is it? When we put some critical pressure on *Phèdre*, we analyse the language of the tragedy, the means by which the tragedy is made and not the tragedy itself. The language of Racinian tragedy has over the years acquired the status of a critical fetish which has frequently gone under the name of 'music', but, once the poetry of Racine is disentangled from the imitation which is the tragedy, then a number of previously disparaged or little-emphasized texts become more helpful to us. The most interesting question to be posed about the music of Racine, however, is not why 300 years of faithful readers suffered from some kind of collective hallucination regarding it, but rather what, exactly, was going under the name of 'music', and why it persisted in doing so for as long as it did. My argument is that this 'music' is the name for what the French seventeenth century called 'figure', and analyses of the opera of Lully and Quinault, as well as of the most famous Alexandrine in all of Racine, 'La fille de Minos et de Pasiphaé', begin to mark out the structure of the figure and its implications for the status of tragic language.

If the first chapter looks into the generalized perception of Racinian music, the second takes up its visual analogue, the Racinian gaze. There is not, I argue, a Racinian gaze, but rather gazes. In addition to the desiring gaze formulated by Jean Starobinski and exemplified by Phèdre's 'ou tel que je vous voi', there is also the Racinian gaze of the hypotyposis, the rhetorical figure which 'sets the thing before the eyes'. This gaze, exemplified by Théramène's 'J'ai vu', is consonant with an emblematic structure of meaning-making, and can be brought into relation with the controversy between the advocates of drawing and the advocates of colour which was engaging the Académie royale de peinture et de sculpture around the time of *Phèdre*'s première. As it happens, the two painters championed by the opposing sides in the controversy, Poussin and Rubens, both treated the death of Hippolytus. Through an analysis of the Poussin and the Rubens treatments of the subject, I argue for a christological model for the *récit de Théramène*. The body of Hippolyte, which is 'sans forme et sans couleur' but nevertheless visible, is a profoundly figural structure, one whose analogue is made visible by Rubens as the nothing and the everything of a litter of shells on the shore, and one in which Racinian language finds its image.

The third chapter turns away from the question of Racinian language and towards the question of Racinian memory. If the language of the tragedy is deeply rooted in an important contemporary conceptual structure, that of the figure, memory in the tragedy also has a contact point which extends the tragedy beyond the stage, causing it to echo and elaborate a determining structure of its own day. This is the labyrinth, both the tragedy's fabled Labyrinth of Crete into which Phèdre fantastically descends in her erotic declaration scene, and the labyrinth which the landscape gardener André Le Nôtre executed for Versailles. Descended as a teacher into a centreless, thread-less labyrinth, in which the monster is never found, and in which memory is held in the perfect Proustian equipoise of 'retrouvée ou perdue', Phèdre treads a maze whose analogue is the horticultural labyrinth in the garden of Versailles: one decorated with thirty-nine fountains meant to teach the morals of Aesop, whose entrance declares the mnemotechnological thread of Ariadne to be useless, and which, in contradistinction to earlier labyrinths in the aristocratic garden, is centreless. This centrelessness changes the mnemodynamics of this originary story of memory and forgetting, and Phèdre's erotic declaration may be read as a function of a contemporary conception of memory and the project of heuristics.

The fourth chapter gathers together the threads which have run through the first three. The Racine *enraciné* which has been sketched out, a Racinian text profoundly rooted in the conceptual structures of its own time and place, is also a text which has ever been radically open to the possibility of being construed. Music for Henri Bremond, gaze for Jean Starobinski, the Racinian text has authorized adultery for Leo Spitzer, has morphed into *Hamlet* for Roland Barthes and has called up Saint George for Charles Mauron. This chapter questions how a text can bear so much critical weight, and the investigation has much in common with the kind of study known as reception history. Whereas the notion of reception history, however, implies a stable object which is then received, I assume rather that the Racinian text can more instructively be conceptualized as having the ontological status of another text grown heavy under the weight of philological inquiry, that of 'Homer'. This chapter, then, takes on the construction of the Racinian text. I prefer this term to some other, such as 'interpretation', or 'constitution', for its etymological meaning: its accent on 'to heap up' (*struere*), and its prefix, 'with, together, jointly'. To construct involves a heaping up with parts, in this case, that part which Auerbach called 'an almost ideal starting point' for philological inquiry (19), the textual passage. And it is a word, like philology itself, which carries its own contrary shadow: that which is constructed is always potentially deconstructed. It is this fragility of construction which is of interest. A construction is an assemblage from within a field of conflicting forces. Some apparatus is necessary for its maintenance.

The final chapter investigates some of those those forces and that apparatus as they relate to the Racinian text. It traces the logic of the critical gesture which transformed the sublime into the classic, and it focuses upon a series of famous texts by Nicolas Boileau, whose Racine was not 'classic' but rather 'sublime', and a series of less famous texts by the abbé whose personal notions of loss and remembrance led to his positing Racine as 'classic'. Pierre-Joseph Thullier, abbé d'Olivet, was responsible for the continuation of Pellisson's history of the French Academy; he translated Cicero and championed the circumflex accent in the 1740 edition of the *Dictionnaire*, yet was plagued with continual troubles with women which were oddly congruent with his scholarly project, and was accused of purloining a manuscript of Racine. But his argument for the classic Racine stumbled. The stumbling block was a single Alexandrine, the one line of *Phèdre* which resisted being conformed either to the sublime, or to the classicizing aesthetic, the Alexandrine which occupied Racine's readers until well past the middle of the eighteenth century, 'Le flot qui l'apporta recule épouvanté', from the *récit de Théramène*. This line is an index into the slippages in the construction of 'Racine'. Not only did it occasion impressive critical gymnastics on the part of the eighteenth century, concerned with conforming it to the classic, but also it became, for Leo Spitzer in the 1940s, a clear demonstration that '*Phèdre* is the ideal type of a baroque tragedy'.[26] This critical gamut built upon the *récit de Théramène* is the focus of my contention that the availability of the Racinian text is a condition of its thematization of the foundation of the canon, which may be understood as a gesture of mourning and the attendant transfiguration of its object: the *récit de Théramène* is the concentrated site of canonicity, a scene of mourning within the general *Trauerspiel* whose object, both there and gone, the dead body of the Prince, functions as the organizing principle of potentially endless discussion.

These, then, are the conclusions of this particular enterprise: Racinian language is figure, Racinian memory is a labyrinthine site, and 'Racine', to paraphrase the young Nietzsche, is an aesthetic judgement, a construction zone. This is not a reading of *Phèdre* in that it does not attempt to add another global interpretation of the story of Phaedra as read by Racine to those interpretations which have accumulated over the centuries. Still less is it a psychology of characters.[27] Rather, it is an analysis of how one particularly numinous cultural object has been perceived to mean, both in its own time, and subsequently.

But the tragic drive towards totality which is always present in the philological project has not been resisted here with complete success. As the year 1999 celebrates the anniversary of the death of Jean Racine, we might note the congruency of this celebration with the imitation which very profoundly is the tragedy, and marvel once again at the spectacular power of loss to generate Racine. The academic birthday party is of little account.[28] But the wake, a party of meaning-making after the fact, offers to us now its intoxications.

Notes to introduction

1. Henri Bremond, *Racine et Valéry. Notes sur l'initiation poétique* (Paris: Grasset, 1931); Stendhal, *Racine et Shakespeare* (1823, 1825) (Geneva: Slatkine, 1986); Roland Barthes, *Sur Racine* (Paris: Seuil, 1963); Lucien Goldmann, *Le Dieu caché. Etude sur la vision tragique du monde dans les Pensées de Pascal et le théâtre de Racine* (Paris: Gallimard, 1955); Igor Stravinsky and Robert Craft, *Dialogues* (Berkeley: University of California Press, 1982).
2. Nicolas Boileau-Despréaux, 'Réflexion X', *Dialogues, réflexions critiques, œuvres diverses*, ed. Charles-H. Boudhours (Paris: Belles Lettres, 1960); Adrien Thomas Perdou de Subligny, *Dissertation sur les tragédies de Phèdre et d'Hippolyte* (Paris: Sercy, 1677).
3. J. F. La Harpe, *Cours de littérature ancienne et moderne* (Paris: Dupont, 1826), viii. 120–1; Théophile Gautier, *Histoire de l'art dramatique en France depuis vingt-cinq ans* (Leipzig: 1858–9) (Geneva: Slatkine, 1968), vi. 78.
4. Pierre-Joseph Thoulier, abbé d'Olivet, *Remarques de grammaire sur Racine* (Paris: Gandouin, 1738); Leo Spitzer, 'The "Récit de Théramène"', in *Linguistics and Literary History. Essays in Stylistics* (1948) (New York: Russell & Russell, 1962).
5. Jean Rohou, *Jean Racine: entre sa carrière, son œuvre, et son Dieu* (Paris: Fayard, 1992).
6. Stendhal, *Racine et Shakespeare*, 285; Paul Claudel, *Conversation sur Jean Racine* (Paris: Gallimard, 1956), 14.
7. Raymond Picard, *La Carrière de Jean Racine* (Paris: Gallimard, 1961); Alain Viala, *Racine. La Stratégie du caméléon* (Paris: Seghers, 1990).
8. David Maskell, *Racine. A Theatrical Reading* (Oxford: Clarendon Press, 1991); Michael Hawcroft, *Word as Action. Racine, Rhetoric, and Theatrical Language* (Oxford: Clarendon Press, 1992); Henry Phillips, *Racine: Language and Theatre* (Durham: University of Durham Press, 1994); Richard Parish, *Racine. The Limits of Tragedy* (Paris, Seattle, Tübingen: PFSCL, 1993).
9. Phillips, *Racine: Language and Theatre*, 139; Roger W. Herzel, 'Racine, Laurent, and the *Palais à volonté*', *PMLA* 108 (1993), 1064–82.
10. Erich Auerbach, *Literary Language and its Public in Late Latin Antiquity and in the Middle Ages*, trans. Ralph Manheim (Princeton: Princeton University Press, 1965), 16.
11. Friedrich Nietzsche, 'Homer and Classical Philology', trans. J. M. Kennedy, *The Complete Works of Friedrich Nietzsche*, ed. Oscar Levy (New York: Russell & Russell, 1964), iii. 170. *Werke. Kritische Gesamtausgabe* (Berlin and New York: Walter de Gruyter, 1982), II, pt. 1, 268–9.
12. William Dwight Whitney (ed.), *The Century Dictionary and Cyclopedia, with a New Atlas of the World. A Work of General Reference in all Departments of Knowledge* (New York: The Century Company, 1889–91).
13. *De nuptiis Philologiae et Mercurii* in *Martianus Capella and the Seven Liberal Arts*, trans. William Harris Stahl and Richard Johnson, with E. L. Burge (New York: Columbia University Press, 1922), ii. 19.
14. See Hans Ulrich Gumbrecht, '"Un Souffle d'Allemagne ayant passé": Friedrich Diez, Gaston Paris, and the Genesis of National Philologies', *Romance Philology* 40 (1986), 1–37.
15. See Stephen Nichols, Jr. (ed.), 'The New Philology', *Speculum* 65 (1990).

16. Quoted in W. D. Whitney (ed.), *The Century Dictionary and Cyclopedia*, s.v. 'philology'. On Müller, see Gerald Graff, *Professing Literature: An Institutional History* (Chicago: University of Chicago Press, 1987), 69–70.
17. Nietzsche speaks of philology's being 'mixed together like a magic potion from the most outlandish liquors, ores, and bones', 'Homer and Classical Philology', 145.
18. Malcolm Bowie, *Lacan* (Cambridge: Harvard University Press, 1991), 11.
19. Stephen Greenblatt, *Shakespearean Negotiations* (Berkeley: University of California Press, 1988), 1.
20. Auerbach, *Literary Language*, 19.
21. For concise statements of this shift, and for the necessary references, see William Weber, 'Beyond Zeitgeist: Recent Work in Music History', *Journal of Modern History* 66 (1994), 321–45; James Wilkinson, 'A Choice of Fictions: Historians, Memory, Evidence', *PMLA* 111 (1996), 80–92.
22. *De nuptiis*, 39.
23. For a summary of the early stages of the culture wars, see Gerald Graff, *Beyond the Culture Wars. How Teaching the Conflicts Can Revitalize American Education* (New York and London: W. W. Norton, 1992); and for speculations on further developments, Joan Dejean, *Ancients Against Moderns. Culture Wars and the Making of a Fin de Siècle* (Chicago and London: University of Chicago Press, 1997).
24. *Transactions of the Philological Society*; *Studies in Philology*; and *Modern Philology*, respectively.
25. See Nichols, 'The New Philology'; Bernard Cerquiglini, *Eloge de la variante. Une Histoire critique de la philologie* (Paris: Seuil, 1988); but cf. Jules Brody, 'Pourquoi la lecture philologique?' in *Nouvelles Lectures de Montaigne* (Paris: Champion, 1994), 107–25.
26. 'The "Récit de Théramène" ', 119. See Amy Wygant, 'Leo Spitzer's Racine', *MLN* 109 (1994), 632–49.
27. See Philipps, *Racine: Language and Theatre*, 141.
28. See H. Carrington Lancaster, 'Nineteen Forty', *PMLA* 54 (1939), 1314–24 for some remarks on Racine's birthday.

CHAPTER 1

Music
Daughter of Minos and Pasiphae

Somewhere in the long course of the reception history of Racine's tragedies, his readers forgot that the tragedy is not equivalent to the collection of lines of poetry which materially constitute it.[1] In Racine's own day, it was clear that the poetics of the tragedy privileged its *muthos*, the myth, action, or fable which was the story that it told. Indeed, one famous report of Racine's compositional practice tells us that 'Quand il avait ainsi lié toutes les scènes entre elles, il disait, "Ma tragédie est faite", comptant le reste pour rien'.[2] The reporter was Racine's youngest son Louis, who, in the 1740s, set down a memoir of his father's life for the benefit of his own son, also named Jean Racine. Louis had been just a boy when his father died in 1699, he had apparently become somewhat dissipated through the years, and he had a number of clear agendas governing his biographical project. Scholars have accordingly dismissed this account as unlikely. In the Pléiade edition of Racine's complete works, which appeared in 1952, Raymond Picard considered it to be a prime example of 'tout le ridicule des racontars de Louis Racine' (i. 965). However, accounts contemporary with Racine's supposed comment echo and confirm it. Under the entry 'corps' in Furetière's *Dictionnaire*, we find: 'On dit aussi d'une pièce de théâtre que le corps en est fait quand on en a fait le dessein, la distribution, et qu'il n'y a plus que les vers à faire'.[3] Racine's own translation of the famous and problematic definition of tragedy in the *Poetics* of Aristotle is consonant with these accounts: 'La tragédie est l'imitation d'une action grave et complète et qui a sa juste grandeur. Cette imitation se fait par un discours, un style, composé pour le plaisir ...' (ii. 919). The Greek which Racine was translating at this point is *hèdusmenôi logôi*, the Latin of the Vettori edition, which he owned, is *condita oratione*;[4] and a recent translation of the *Poetics* gives the phrase as 'au moyen d'un langage relevé d'assaisonnements d'espèces variées'.[5] The translators justify their rather literal rendering of the term by pointing out that, although the verb *hèdunô* can indeed have the general sense of 'to make pleasant', it is also the usual term for the addition to food of seasonings meant to make it taste better (193–4). This is reflected in the Latin 'conditus', whose first meaning is 'seasoned food'.[6] In the Greek and Latin 'seasoned language', there lurks a theory of tragic language: it would consist of some basic material to which something supplemental is added in order to make it not just palatable, but also pleasurable. It follows that the tragedy and its language are non-identical: there is tragedy, as in 'ma tragédie est faite', and there is the means by which one makes tragedy, its language, concerning which we only know that its purpose is pleasure.

So, incredible as it may seem to ears attuned to the Alexandrine, tragedy for Racine was probably something closer to the prose sketch which we have from him for an *Iphigénie en Tauride* than it was to the glorious poetry of *Iphigénie en Aulide*. This plan in prose for the first act, which reads so woodenly, is an example of the tragedy's design, its distribution, and those lovely Alexandrines which have fascinated from that day to this, have the status of nothing ('rien'), a left-over ('le reste'). In spite of this fact, or perhaps because of it, commentators upon the tragedies have made a fetish of Racinian language. The vocabulary that this fetish has usually adopted is that of the musical: singing, harmony, lyric, and so on. One recent biographer writes of *Phèdre* in terms that evoke the great late-romantic symphonists: 'C'est composé comme une symphonie: thèmes amorcés, thèmes repris, grands airs qui se répondent; et contrepoint aussi, dans le style'.[7] Picard's Pléiade edition seems to claim that the language of *Iphigénie* could have been spoken by Mozart: 'Surtout la consistance verbale a ici la souplesse inflexible de la musique. [...] Avec ses douceurs recueillies d'*adagio*, ses déchaînements de *molto agitato*, ses certitudes glorieuses de *rondo*, la tragédie se déroule comme une sonate ou un oratorio' (i. 685). Lytton Strachey once tuned in to Racine, and dreamed of his voice:

> His music, to ears that are attuned to hear it, comes fraught with a poignancy of loveliness whose peculiar quality is shared by no other poetry in the world. To have grown familiar with the voice of Racine, to have realized once and for all its intensity, its beauty, and its depth, is to have learnt a new happiness, to have discovered something exquisite and splendid, to have enlarged the glorious boundaries of art.[8]

Is this, then, some generalized fantasm? In what follows I shall be seeking a properly early modern answer to a double question: if the language of the tragedy is not the tragedy itself, then what is it? Is this 'nothing', as has been claimed by Racine's readers from that day to this, 'music'?

By no means did the critical obsession with the music of Racine begin, as we might guess, in the wake of Mallarmé. When we turn to the motley crew of satiric, nostalgic, and dissipated observers who left their personal impressions of Jean Racine, it becomes clear that it was the sound of him that fascinated and remained. Racine possessed in the highest degree a skill which has since suffered an almost total decline: the skill of reading aloud. Long after Racine's death, Valincourt, his successor in the Academy and as royal historiographer, undertook to set down some impressions of him for the abbé d'Olivet's continuation of Pellisson's history of the Académie française.[9] He claims still to see Racine reading before him:

> Je me souviens à ce sujet qu'étant un jour à Auteuil chez Despréaux avec M. Nicole et quelques autres amis d'un mérite distingué, nous mîmes Racine sur l'Oedipe de Sophocle: et il s'émeut à un tel point, que tout ce que nous étions d'auditeurs, nous éprouvâmes tous les sentiments de terreur et de compassion, sur quoi roule cette tragédie. J'ai vu nos meilleurs acteurs sur le théâtre, j'ai entendu nos meilleures pièces; mais jamais rien n'approcha du trouble où me jeta ce récit: et au moment même que je vous écris, je m'imagine voir encore Racine avec son livre à la main, et nous tous consternés autour de lui.

'Il possédoit au suprême degré le talent de la déclamation', Valincourt continues. Racine was apt to read with passion and fire not only the lines of others, but also his own. Indeed, it was his compositional practice to pronounce his lines aloud as he composed them:

> C'étoit même assez sa coutume de déclamer ses vers avec feu, à mesure qu'il les composait. Il m'a plusieurs fois conté que pendant qu'il faisoit sa tragédie de Mithridate, il alloit tous les matins aux Tuilleries, où travailloient alors toutes sortes d'ouvriers; et que récitant ses vers à haute voix, sans s'apercevoir seulement qu'il y eût personne dans le jardin, tout à coup il s'y trouva environné de tous ces ouvriers. Ils avoient quitté leur travail pour le suivre, le prenant pour un homme qui par désespoir alloit se jeter dans le bassin. (336)

This widely acknowledged talent for declamation—Louis Racine was to write, 'Tout le monde sait le talent que mon père avait pour la déclamation' ('Mémoires', 58)—brings us to the problem of the musicality of Racine's tragic language, for the style of declamation current in the seventeenth century and for a long time thereafter was widely perceived as a kind of singing.[10] Until well past the middle of the nineteenth century, declamation and singing were understood to occupy one side of a performance practice, the other side of which was speech. And, according to a certain tradition, the voice of Racine was linked quite literally to the tragic stage: it is variously reported that he personally taught the art of declamation to the greatest tragic actress of the day, Mlle de Champmeslé, line by line. It is further alleged that when Jean-Baptiste Lully wished to create an operatic recitative style suited to the French language, he studied the declamation of La Champmeslé in order to get his melody and accents right: 'On prétend qu'il alloit le [le récitatif] former à la Comedie sur les tons de la Chanmêlé. Il écoutoit déclamer la Chanmêlé, retenoit ses tons, puis leûr donnoit grace, l'harmonie & le degré de force qu'ils devoient avoir dans la bouche d'un Chanteur, pour convenir à la Musique à laquelle il les aproprioit de cette maniere.'[11] There exist important reasons for believing neither in the link between the voice of La Champmeslé and the operatic stage, nor in the role of the great tragic actress as the median term in a productive practice which begins with the voice of Racine and ends with Lully. As for the former, the Comtesse who has reported Lully's practice in this passage from Le Cerf's dialogue, claims that Lully found inspiration for an *air de violon* in the hoofbeats of his horse, and, for the lament of Pan from *Isis*, in the sound of the wind itself. What is at stake in the passage, accordingly, is probably not, or not mainly, accuracy with respect to event. Rather, what seems to matter is Lully's ability to 'imiter la nature', and so to have merit as a composer. As for Racine's teaching declamation to La Champmeslé, the evidence for this claim was long ago weighed, and found wanting.[12] Certainly, La Champmeslé was already an accomplished actress before she ever met Racine. Further, Louis Racine, to whom the claim may be traced, clearly had an agenda in reporting it: he was attempting to use it as a means for denying his father's love affair with the actress ('Mémoires', 58–9). This is not conclusively to say that La Champmeslé did not accept Racine's tutelage with respect to declamation, but rather only to point out that the little tale is at least somewhat improbable and may well have led a life of its own, independent of any event.

But it is precisely this independent life which can potentially be led by anecdote which is of interest here. What is at stake in the discussion of the musicality of Racinian language is not whether it is or is not in some absolute sense. Rather, what we can know of the situation is that it has been perceived to be so at various times and places; we can know the stories that have been told. Clearly, Racine's contemporaries and immediate posterity wanted to connect his voice to the operatic stage through the medium of La Champmeslé. What was perceived was a connection at a level far more basic than that at which the polemic against the opera by Racine and Boileau was being conducted. The connection between opera and tragedy was being perceived to function at the level of the voice itself, in a literal translation of the voice of Racine first on to the stage, and then from the stage of musical declamation to the stage of declamatory music.

The lyricism and the harmony of this voice became an embattled quality in the eighteenth century. In his enthusiasm, Voltaire is said to have recommended writing at the bottom of each of his predecessor's pages, 'Beau! pathétique! harmonieux! sublime!'[13] Yet Diderot cites Garrick to the effect that when the actor on the stage was 'enlacé par les vers harmonieux de [Racine], comme par autant de serpents dont les replis lui étreignent la tête, les pieds, les mains, les jambes et les bras, son action perdrait toute sa liberté'.[14] While La Harpe claimed Racine for 'le premier rang de nos poètes lyriques'—'On ne trouvera point dans notre langue une poésie plus véritablement lyrique, une harmonie plus diversifiée et plus musicale'[15]—the nineteenth-century history of Racinian musicality includes a chapter in which the voice of Racine was widely perceived explicitly to be a prose voice: a voice embodied in the slight figure of the actress responsible for the great mid-century revival of the tragic stage, Rachel Félix. The performance practice of Rachel was summed up by Alfred de Musset as 'elle ne déclame point, elle parle'.[16]

But it is to the twentieth century that we may look both for the highest pitch of controversy concerning Racinian musicality, and for the only faithful answer to the question of the status of Racinian language. The controversy swirled around a single line from *Phèdre*, the most famous periphrasis in all of French literature, 'La fille de Minos et de Pasiphaé', from act I, scene 1.

In France, 'la fille de Minos et de Pasiphaé' was launched by Gonzague Truc in the 1915 *Revue d'histoire littéraire de la France.*[17]

Truc's estimation of 'La "nouveauté" dans la langue de Racine' is that there isn't any, and that any innovatory force in his language resides in the 'alliance des mots' (137), and not in their novelty as such.

> Il lui suffit d'assembler des noms pour créer de l'harmonie: La fille de Minos et de Pasiphaé. ... Evidemment il faut prendre chaque mot dans son sens plein, dans sa valeur étymologique, saisir la raison de l'enchaînement des propositions, et de la distribution des épithètes. Mais l'intelligence de notre idiome classique est à ce prix, et à nous la coulpe si la croissante désorganisation du français ne nous permet plus d'en saisir la nature intime à sa plus belle époque. (139)

Whatever is harmonious about this Alexandrine, Truc asserts, lodges in the proper names. But that harmony is not explained; Truc cites the line as though its harmony were self-evident. We can read it only by grasping the fullness of meaning of each of its words, which is identical with etymological value, and by seizing the rationale of their combination and distribution. Meaning, reason, and intelligence are the key words here. If we cannot grasp the intimate nature of the French language, which is at this time growing increasingly disorganized, the fault is our own. Truc is not going to tell us what its harmony is: we must pay a price for this seizure of the French language. Truc's 'nous'—'à nous la coulpe'—is later specified as 'fils impénitents des romantiques' (145), and his point is finally hortatory. 'We' must return to Racine, and specifically to his harmonious manipulation of words which are themselves in no way innovative, 'pour apprendre à travailler' (146). We learn from Racine that 'la nouveauté dans le style vient plutôt de la sourde élaboration du génie, que du frivole désir de cacher sous l'imprévu ou l'hétéroclite de la forme, la pénurie de l'intelligence et du sentiment' (146). There can be no doubt about the use to which the perception of harmony is here being put. 'La fille de Minos et de Pasiphaé' has become a bulwark against a threatening linguistic disorganization, characterized as the frivolous desire to hide behind generally unforeseen and heteroclite form. This line is a dividing line. Either its harmony can be perceived and one does not suffer from poverty of intelligence and sentiment, or it cannot be perceived, and all is lost.

What is old about Truc's formulation is the positioning of Racine as the bane of the romantic imagination. Whether this is essential and healthy, as he seems to be saying, or noxious and politically reactionary, as Stendhal had insisted,[18] the constellation itself is almost a hundred years old by 1915. What is new here is the plucking of this particular Alexandrine out of the Racinian corpus in order to suggest that there is something special about it which goes under the name of 'harmonie', but which remains all suggestion and nuance, and in order to use it as a litmus test in a general discussion of contemporary literary production. That the 'élaboration du génie' to which it is an index should be characterized as mysterious, hidden, and secret, 'sourde', mutes our line and restricts to the sharp-eared initiate the hearing of its delicate harmony.

The twentieth-century discussion of this Alexandrine was bilingual. Before Truc and his muting of 'La fille' in order to combat the forces of novelty in the French language, Lytton Strachey, in his essay on Racine dating from 1908, had insisted upon the line as exemplary of the sounding quality of Racinian language. 'When we come across the mysterious accent of fatality and remote terror in a single perfectly simple phrase—"La fille de Minos et de Pasiphaé"—we are apt not to hear that it is there.'[19] In this essay which is permeated with references to the visual music of Racine—'It is as if we had become so accustomed to looking at boxers, wrestlers, and gladiators that the sight of an exquisite minuet produced no effect on us' (13)—it is nevertheless clear that Strachey intends 'to hear' literally. 'In a sense we can know him in our library, just as we can hear the music of Mozart with silent eyes. But, when the strings begin, when the whole volume of that divine harmony engulfs us, how differently then we understand and feel!' (28) For Strachey, Racinian language still manifests itself as a voice. His closing argument is that that language must be heard on the stage in order to be experienced properly, and there is some possibility that the voice of Sarah Bernhardt is that ideal embodiment. She had taken her troupe to England for the first time in the summer of 1879, and among the British for whom she was a revelation was the young Oscar Wilde. Following her opening-night performance, he remarked, 'It was not until I heard Sarah Bernhardt in *Phèdre* that I realized the sweetness of the music of Racine.'[20]

In France, it was the critic and historian Henri Bremond, who had long lived in England, who next considered 'La fille' to be exemplary. The discussion which he initiated was pursued in significant part in the pages of *The New York Times*.

In his 1931 *Racine et Valéry. Notes sur l'initiation poétique*,[21] Bremond claimed that he might well have called his book 'Racine et la poésie pure', or 'Racine et Edgar Poe', or 'Racine et Mallarmé', or even 'Racine et M. Bradley' (xii). Even after discovering that Bremond held A. C. Bradley, Professor of Poetry at Oxford from 1901 to 1905, in high regard particularly for his inaugural lecture, 'Poetry for Poetry's Sake',[22] we might still wonder at this series of couplings with the name of Racine. What was the logic in Bremond's assimilation of Racine to 'la poésie pure'?

Bremond claimed that the problem of 'la poésie pure' was first suggested to him in 1920. It was his reading of Valéry's avant-propos to the collection of Lucien Fabre, *Connaissance de la déesse*, 'qui réveillait chez moi [...] l'angoisse de ce problème, en nous invitant à creuser la notion de la poésie pure'.[23] Elected to the Académie française in 1923, Bremond in the autumn of 1925 gave the annual address to the plenary session of the Institute, and his subject was 'La Poésie pure'. His argument begins with an observation about the 'novelty' which had so disturbed Gonzague Truc: 'Les modernes théoriciens de la poésie pure, Edgar Poe, Baudelaire, Mallarmé, M. Paul Valéry ne sont pas les dangereux novateurs que parfois l'on semble croire.'[24] Bremond argues that these theorists advocate not novelty but rather 'poésie-musique', as opposed to 'poésie-raison' (25). But this music is emphatically not of the sounding variety: 'Grelots de la rime, flux et reflux des allitérations, cadences tour à tour prévues ou dissonantes, aucun de ces jolis bruits ne parvient jusqu'à la zone profonde où fermente l'inspiration, où l'on ne perçoit, avec le Périclès de Shakespeare, que la musique des sphères' (25). Rather, the words of poetry transmit a 'fluide mystérieux' (26); they are 'conducteurs qui doivent leur sonorité même et leur splendeur éphémère au courant qui les traverse' (26). 'Ce sont des talismans, ou des sortilèges, des gestes ou des formules magiques, des charmes au sens premier de ce mot. Simple harmonie et nouée au sens dans la prose, cette musique verbale devient, dès qu'elle s'est imposée au poète, une véritable incantation' (26). This music of poetry surpasses the simple harmony of prose, which is linked to meaning. Leaving meaning behind at the level of simple harmony, verbal music jumps from harmony to magic formula, and, in a final leap, using Walter Pater as a springboard, explicitly aspires to rejoin prayer: 'S'il en faut croire Walter Pater, "tous les arts aspireraient à rejoindre la musique". Non, ils aspirent tous, mais chacun par les magiques intermédiaires qui lui sont propres,—les mots; les notes; les couleurs; les lignes;—ils aspirent tous à rejoindre la prière' (27).

Bremond's Institute address served as the starting point for a series of barbed commentaries which he exchanged with the literary critic of *Le Temps* and Paris literary correspondent for *The New York Times*, Paul Souday (1869–1929), on the subject of 'la poésie pure'. Bremond was, so he claimed, misunderstood, and he began shortly to publish in the *Nouvelles littéraires* a series of 'éclaircissements'. In the first of these, 'M. Paul Souday ou le martyr de la poésie-raison',[25] 'La fille' first appeared as an example of 'la poésie pure':

Avec tous ceux qui lisent poétiquement les poètes, j'avais remarqué que, pour sentir le charme d'un vers, d'un lambeau de vers, pas n'est besoin de connaître le poème où ce vers, ce lambeau se trouvent [*sic*].

La fille de Minos et de Pasiphaë

'Exagération', me répond M. Souday. 'Si vous ne saviez pas qui sont le père et la mère de Phèdre', ces magiques syllabes vous laisseraient froid. ... Cette généalogie le met en extase. Nous autres pas. Quand je vous disais que nous n'habitons pas le même monde! (36–7)

Bremond, then, did two things to advance the career of 'La fille'. Firstly, like Truc, he considered the line to be a dividing line, and here it was indeed a battle line. But Bremond caused 'La fille' to cross over that line. It no longer served Truc's argument for understanding poetry, for grasping its meaning. Rather, it now served the forces of whatever in poetry is not meaning, the forces of 'poésie-musique'. Secondly, Bremond took Truc's muting of Racinian language one step further. By shattering the Racinian text and claiming that the line might exist in its full poetic adequacy as a fragment, Bremond created the Racinian sound bite. But it was a silent sound bite, and, in the first of his three citations of the line in the later *Racine et Valéry*, it escaped ever further from any potential manifestation in the sound-world, as

La fille de Mineos [*sic*] et de Pamphaë [*sic*] (142).

While Strachey had insisted upon Racine as the sound of Mozart, the Racinian Mozartian music which interested Bremond was the unheard: 'Deux musiques chez Racine comme chez Mozart: celle qui frappe directement les oreilles; celle qu'à proprement parler nous n'entendons pas' (179).

Common to Truc and Bremond is what might be called a lack of analysis. Truc never explained what exactly it was about the meaning of 'La fille' which he considered to be so harmonious; neither did Bremond ever discuss what he called its music in specific terms.

Indeed, he explicitly claimed in *Racine et Valéry* that the definition of the song of Racine is that it cannot be defined: 'Celui-ci échappe invinciblement, et par définition, à nos facultés critiques' (182).

My project is not to judge these discussions adversely because they appear to be unanalytical. Henri Bremond considered this entire literary-critical excursion to be precisely that: a mere clausula within his eleven-volume *Histoire littéraire du sentiment religieux en France depuis la fin des guerres de réligion jusqu'à nos jours*.[26] He considered his life work to be a systematic inquiry into 'la vie intérieure, sur l'action de la grâce dans les âmes'. And his project was to discuss not so much pure poetry as pure prayer. His was a careful apology for all true mystics, among whom he counted himself. If you are not a member of 'la religion de Racine' (129), you cannot convert. 'La fille de Minos et de Pasiphaé' became a sacrament.

The discussion went round and round. Souday summed up its opening salvos in the 29 November 1925 *New York Times Book Review* article, 'Poe and the Theory of Pure Poetry'.

> M. l'Abbé Bremond is a pure mystic and treats reason like a personal enemy, relying only upon inspiration from on high. [...] He professes that only the sound of verse determines the poetic impression, and that its meaning has absolutely no importance. In fact, he is absolutely wrong. The verses which he quoted as examples, especially those formed of proper names like Racine's "Phedre" [*sic*]:
>
> La fille de Minos et de Pasiphae [*sic*],
>
> move us even when we don't know who those personages are, only because the sounds evoke the idea of terrible or charming beings.

Souday neglected all the nuance of Bremond's thought, misstated Bremond's position on the sound of poetry, and additionally misquoted Racine for his American readers. But what truly outraged him was Bremond's 'mysterious fluid', which he did not misunderstand, nor did it escape him that Bremond's main interest was in God:

> He [Bremond] concludes that pure poetry consists of a 'mysterious fluid' which transfigures the 'words void of sense or in which the sense is trivial', and which puts us in communion with the infinite, or even with God.
>
> But no one knows what this 'mysterious fluid' is, and no one will believe that God employs only 'meaningless words' with which to communicate with his creatures. [...] What gives words their poetic value is not such electro-magnetic 'currents'; it is the immaterial, rational harmony of verbal music and of thought, as Poe so transcendently realized.

What comes through in this passage is a popular rage against the paradox which lodged itself at the heart of Bremond's thought, and perhaps at the heart of all true mysticism. It is the paradoxical situation that poetry is unparaphrasable, it cannot be re-expressed in terms other than its own, words (Bremond's 'discours') are inadequate to it; and yet at the same time words are its medium, and we have only words, and perhaps the very same words which make up 'discours', as a way of knowing it. Bremond was not uncourageous when it came to stating this paradox baldly, and he stated it in terms of 'La fille':

L'harmonieux Racine, dit-on ...

La fille de Minos et de Pasiphaé ...

Sans doute, mais cette harmonie prise en elle-même et au sens qu'on lui donne communément, n'a rien où la prose ne puisse prétendre: c'est une qualité du style, ou, ce qui revient ici au même, du discours. [...] Il faut cependant que le *discours* du poète rejoigne ce *chant* mystérieux dont parle Valéry, et qui est pour nous la poésie même: un chant, remarquez-le, que, d'un côté, aucun mot ne peut *exprimer*, sans quoi il redescendrait au rang du discours; et qu'il faut bien, d'un autre côté, que le discours, que les mots nous transmettent, puisque, n'entendant que des mots, nous nous éveillons, nous nous accordons à un chant. (179–80)

A certain congruency of structure should alert us here to the presence of a difficult, but properly seventeenth-century notion: the structure, 'chant-discours' is analogous to the structure which the French seventeenth century called 'figure'. Characterized by simultaneous presence and absence, satisfaction and desire, this is the 'figure' whose history was once delineated by Auerbach,[27] and which Louis Marin has developed with respect to the *Pensées* of Pascal.[28]

It is unclear why exactly Souday refused to stare into the heart of Bremond's paradox, and why it made him so furious, whether he was fundamentally disturbed by all paradox, or whether it was just this one which struck him as absurd.[29] Perhaps Bremond's unhappy formulation of the 'mysterious fluid' was simply too tempting a target. But, whatever their motivation, Souday's comments constitute a refusal which characterized the subsequent discussion of the musicality of Racinian language and of 'La fille' in particular. Without coming to terms with Bremond's insight into that language as 'figure', the discussion could only chase its own tail, and degenerate into a 'Yes, it is; no, it isn't' argument. Some either lament or celebrate Racine's musicality, misunderstood as sounding language; some contend that his lines are more important for their meaning. 'La fille de Minos et de Pasiphaë', André Malraux wrote, '...n'est pas une indication biographique.'[30] But those who leaned more to the side of meaning, misunderstood as referentiality, produced a new generation of biographies and historical notices concerning Racine. In 1926, Gonzague Truc published his biography, *Jean Racine: l'œuvre, l'artiste, l'homme et le temps*,[31] and, in the 15 January 1928 issue of the *Mercure*, Jean Demeure exploded the story of 'les quatre amis de *Psyché*'. Also in 1928, Mauriac's *La Vie de Jean Racine* appeared from Plon.

And so, in a final distant echo of the position taken up by Souday, Raymond Picard, in the Pléiade edition, combined the two complementary misunderstandings of Bremond's vision, and was able to insist on the justification of this now extremely famous Alexandrine as not only sound, but also something more than sound. This was indeed, and additionally, an 'indication biographique': 'La richesse de ce vers n'est pas seulement musicale, comme on l'a tant répété. Racine ne se serait peut-être pas permis une périphrase injustifiée, fût-elle la plus mélodieuse du monde. Mais dans une action où la fatalité du sang joue un si grand rôle, il fallait marquer dès le début la filiation funeste de Phèdre' (i. 1168).

One senses a kind of critical exhaustion in this comment: 'comme on l'a tant répété'. It is an exhaustion which was produced by the potentially endless critical circling around a hollow centre. Henri Bremond had, almost singlehandedly, made 'La fille de Minos et de Pasiphaé' into the most famous song of Racine. But his rationale for doing so was, paradoxically, mystic. Subtract that mysticism, while retaining its terms, and the result is a critical practice trapped within an exhausted notion of what it means to mean.

This brief history of the musicality of Racinian language suggests that something radical, in both senses, happened to that quality in the twentieth century. Both a radical break, and a return to a certain kind of root occurred. What Bremond accomplished, besides creating a great deal of confusion, was the disjunction of Racinian language and the voice. In order for 'La fille' to be considered 'musical', it necessarily had to remain unheard. A sound event in England, the musical in Bremond's thought was silent, the site of his paradoxical, figural reading of Racinian language. Bremond's central insight was misunderstood, parodied, or simply ignored, but his terminology was nevertheless taken up with a vengeance and 'La fille' became the example of a musicality which, for Bremond's successors in the discussion, sounded aloud again.

Having initiated the discussion, Bremond died in 1933, leaving his *Histoire* unfinished, and leaving Valéry himself to regret having ever mentioned the notion of 'la poésie pure'.[32] With respect to Racine, it seems to have been subsequently quite impossible to discuss his theatre without choosing sides. Either one valorized the sound envelope or one valorized the referentiality. At most, as in the opinion hazarded by Picard, the meaning of Racinian language was considered to be a combination of the two. Never was the combinatorial seriously questioned. On the contrary, it was eternalized, and it was this eternalization which the *Nouvelle critique* would later challenge. The accomplishment of Roland Barthes, Charles Mauron, and Lucien Goldmann was nothing less than the redefinition of what it means to mean. Racine was the battleground of this redefinition because whatever was going under the name of the 'musical' in his tragic language had become the site of this constructed eternalization.

At issue here is the way in which a particular paradox, the paradox of 'silent music', is understood. Whereas the successors of Henri Bremond simply torched the paradox and recast the discussion in terms of the combinatorial, Bremond's immersion in seventeenth-century mysticism led him to a properly seventeenth-century understanding of the status of tragic language. If we can understand Racinian language as 'figure', then we will have some knowledge of a much broader cultural stance, and an index into that language's flickering, its fetish status and its fantasy.

'Figure porte absence et présence, plaisir et déplaisir.'[33] If it is the case that the lines of poetry which collectively represent the tragedy of Racine do precisely that—that is, they represent, in the sense that the figural does—then the poetics of our famous Alexandrine should reveal signs of this structure.

Much of the phonic weight of the line seems to rest upon the proper names: with respect to sheer time-value, exactly half of the line is expended on proper naming. *Phèdre* as a whole might be called Racine's tragedy of the Name: more proper names appear in *Phèdre* than in any of the preceding tragedies. There are 45 in all, and the first scene of the first act is the concentrated site of this procedure, containing 33 proper names. In one passage of 13 lines (81–93), there are 14. Irrespective of any specific referentiality, the sheer sound value of the proper name from antiquity was not lost upon seventeenth-century prosody. Boileau's *L'art poétique* offers this formulation:

La fable offre à l'esprit mille agréments divers:
Là, tous les noms heureux semblent nés pour les vers,
Ulysse, Agamemnon, Oreste, Idoménée,
Hélène, Ménélas, Pâris, Hector, Enée.
Ô le plaisant projet d'un poète ignorant,
Qui de tant de héros va choisir Childebrand!
D'un seul nom quelquefois le son dur ou bizarre
Rend un poème entier, ou burlesque ou barbare. (iii. 237–44)

It would seem that there are two kinds of proper name sounds. Firstly, there are those, drawn from Greek and Latin antiquity, which are somehow born to the poetic line. They group themselves naturally into Alexandrines and their rhyme is not only rich (defined as homophony not only between the last accented vowels but also between the consonants preceding them) but rather more than rich: 'Enée' entire effortlessly echoes 'Idoménée'. Born to poetry here means not just born to metre, but, especially, born to that ornament which becomes a general metonymy for poetry itself, rhyme.[34]

This *tour de force* of the antique name, however, may be contrasted with the example, drawn from French medieval history, of the name whose sound is intrinsically difficult. 'Childebrand' is an unhappy choice for the subject of a poem because of the sound of his name, which can be made to rhyme with 'ignorant'.[35] The problem which is thrown into relief by the rhyme is the consonant preceding the rhyme, the 'b' of '-brand'. This hateful 'b' then proceeds to infect the next two lines of the poem, just as Boileau happens to be claiming at this moment it is capable of doing, as the 'bizarre', 'burlesque', and 'barbare'. There are two kinds of proper name sounds, then: those native to verse, as indicated by their easy homophony, a homophony which is self-contained and does not tend to infection; and those which rhyme with embarrassing words like 'ignorant', and which tend to spread through whole poems, destroying them like viruses.

In spite of the fact that Racine was dealing in the first scene of *Phèdre* only with names drawn from 'la fable', it seems that he was nevertheless sensitive to this distinction. It may have been something unacceptable about the sound of the name of the outlaw 'Périphètès', for example, which produced the periphrasis, 'géant d'Épidaure', in line 84. But for the rest, there is a certain exaltation in this first scene at the glorious homophony of these proper names, which is demonstrated here, as it had been in Boileau's technical example, by placing them at the ends of lines, in the position of rhyme-words.

With one exception, this is most uniformly the case with the names of the main characters in the play.

Phèdre begins with a proper-name rhyme:

> Le dessein en est pris: je pars, cher Théramène,
> Et quitte le séjour de l'aimable Trézène. (1–2)

and proceeds to supply at least one rhyme for the name of each remaining major character: abusée–Thésée (21–2); méprisée–Thésée (61–2); opposée–Thésée (125–6); ennemie–Aricie (49–50); adoucie–Aricie (101–2); fuite–Hippolyte (57–8). And, lest anyone should have missed the phonic point of the procedure, the scene frames itself by concluding on one final name rhyme: ordonne–Œnone (141–2). A complicated problem begins to be suggested by this list: the second word of the rhyme is linked to the first by something other than homophony. 'Ennemie' and 'adoucie', for example, mark out the limits of the status of the character of Aricie in the plot. 'Fuite', as has frequently been remarked, is going to be the one and only movement of the character of Hippolyte: his role is to escape the stage. A contrast could be drawn with the theory of the Parnassian poets, as formulated by Théodore de Banville: 'Vous ferez rimer ensemble, autant qu'il se pourra, des mots très semblables entre eux comme son, et très différents entre eux comme sens.'[36] For Racine, on the other hand, it seems that the ideal is not the 'rime-surprise' of the Parnassian poets, but rather a 'rime-sécurité'.[37] That is, the rhymed proper name as a metonymy for a character complex begins to mark out and secure that character complex, lending it either impetus ('fuite'), or range ('ennemie'–'adoucie'), or pathos ('méprisée', 'opposée', 'abusée'), or even, perhaps, irony ('ordonne').

All of which makes it even more startling and disturbing that the one exception to what could be called in the broadest sense the rhyme scheme of the tragedy is the proper name of Phèdre. It has been noted that, when Racine invents a character, the invented name will most often rhyme with the character whose confidant, friend, or lover he/she is. Examples of this would be Achille–Eriphile from *Iphigénie*, Albine–Agrippine from *Britannicus*, Cléone–Hermione from *Andromaque*, Phoedime-Monime from *Mithridate*.[38] If this observation has any force, then it would have to be said that there is a rhyme crisis in *Phèdre*. 'Phèdre' rhymes with nothing. It rhymes with no other proper name of a main character, and Racine did not seize the day with respect to Panope, Phèdre's handmaiden.

Not only does 'Phèdre' not rhyme with any other proper name of a character; neither does it rhyme with any other word in the Racinian store of rhymes.[39] Apparently unrhymable, the name of Phèdre is thus unavailable to the technique of the 'rime-sécurité', a technique which is one of the most subtle and suggestive in the repertoire of the tragedy. The impossibility of *Phèdre*, we might then say, on the level of the sound of its language, is that the name of its protagonist come at the end of a line, that it suggest its own definition by its homophony or consonance, that it be to itself its own sound-world, that it be, in short, born to rhyme. With respect to sound, 'Phèdre' is far closer to 'Childebrand' than she is to 'Enée'. The sound of 'Phèdre' places her not among the mellifluous ancients, but rather among the French.

The name of Phèdre is thus conspicuous by its absence from the rhyme scheme of the tragedy. Like the dramatic device of delaying the entrance of the star until well into the action of the play, the absence of the name of Phèdre from the rhyme scheme makes the end of the Alexandrine a sensitive and suspenseful place. 'La fille de Minos et de Pasiphaé' is accordingly not just a periphrasis at the level of the referentiality of the expression. It does indeed stand in the place of 'Phèdre' with respect to its meaning. But it is doubly periphrastic: both in the register of meaning and in the register of sound the name of Phèdre has been replaced. From the eighteenth century on, the appropriateness of the former has been remarked. Concerning it, Louis Racine wrote, 'Ce n'est pas sans dessein que le poète instruit de la naissance de Phèdre. Comme fille de Minos, elle doit aimer la vertu; comme fille de Pasiphaé, il n'est pas étonnant qu'elle soit susceptible d'une passion honteuse.'[40] But the latter replacement is more necessary and urgent. The problem is not the pronunciation of the name; 'Phèdre' is pronounced five times in this first scene alone. Rather, the problem is the rhyme. So, the technique of this sound-replacement must inevitably place its accent on the rhyme-word, the proper name of Phèdre's mother, Pasiphaé. Concerning the line's sound envelope, Louis's comment was, 'Le nom propre peut faire excuser cette rime' (143). Why, we might well wonder, are excuses necessary?

'Envoyé' and 'Pasiphaé' constitue only a 'rime pauvre', a rhyme, that is, in which only the final vowels participate. Indeed, since the rhyming vowel is not followed by a consonant, this phonic link might equally be called assonance.[41] The rhyme-status of the name of

Phèdre's mother seems accordingly, like that of her daughter, to place her closer to Childebrand, among the barbarous rather than among the mellifluous ancients. But the poverty of rhyme, Louis seems to be saying, is excused by the very impossibility of rhyming this proper name in any other way: it flirts with total unrhymability because it infringes upon the one rule which seventeenth-century prosody set itself in the matter of poetic sound. This name, 'd'une sonorité à la fois si douce et si étrange' (Cahan, 138), breaks the rule against the hiatus. The hiatus is the juxtaposition of two vowels, or two diphthongs, or a vowel and a diphthong, other than *e muet*. 'Ami estimable' has a hiatus between the two words; 'amie estimable' does not. Boileau warns against this hole between vowels in *L'art poétique*:

> Gardez qu'une voyelle à courir trop hâtée
> Ne soit d'une voyelle en son chemin heurtée. (i. 107–8)

Exemplary of the need ever to watch Boileau very closely, each one of these lines contains a hiatus for the ear, between the penultimate word and the rhyme-word. However, the vowels are separated by unpronounced consonants, and, technically, no hiatus has been committed. Phonic satire: the law of poetic sound can be circumvented by orthography. 'Dire' bows to 'voir' even in the matter of the law proper to it.

Accordingly, the name of Phèdre's mother may indeed have sounded strange and foreign to a seventeenth-century ear, but because of its internal hiatus, it would precisely not have sounded 'douce' or musical or harmonious, or have been considered to be exemplary of any such quality as we have been noting here was and is generally considered characteristic of the poetic language of Racine. As sound, it is faulty, and it is precisely the presence of this fault which excuses, Louis Racine seems to be saying, a rhyme which is so barely satisfactory as to point up its own borderline unrhymability.

On the subject of the rhyme, *L'art poétique* is explicit:

> Quelque sujet qu'on traite, ou plaisant, ou sublime,
> Que toujours le bon sens s'accorde avec la rime:
> L'un l'autre vainement ils semblent se haïr;
> La rime est une esclave, et ne doit qu'obéir. (i. 27–30)

But what does it mean that in this very passage, which was originally published together with Boileau's translation of the *On the Sublime* of 'Longinus', the word 'sublime' rhymes with 'rime'? What is secured by this 'rime-sécurité', if such it is, would be identity, if only an underground one, between the sublime and the rhyme, in the same way as an identity of 'Hippolyte' is marked out by the rhyme with 'fuite'. This identity suggests a counter-current to the thinking marked by the slave metaphor. That counter-current suggests not only that sense and sound, meaning and rhyme, are mutually determining, but also that the sublime rhyme exercises control over sense. Voltaire formulated the problem in this way:

> Donner aux auteurs de nouvelles rimes, ce serait leur donner de nouvelles pensées, car l'assujettissement à la rime fait que souvent on ne trouve dans la langue qu'un seul mot qui puisse finir un vers: on ne dit presque jamais ce qu'on voulait dire; on ne peut se servir du mot propre; on est obligé de chercher une pensée pour la rime, parce qu'on ne peut trouver de rime pour exprimer ce que l'on pense.[42]

Friedrich Schiller, who undertook a translation of *Phèdre* in 1804, wrote to his friend Goethe in 1799: 'The characteristic division of the Alexandrine into two equal halves, and the nature of the rhyme, which forms every two Alexandrines into a couplet, determines not only the entire language, but also the entire inner spirit of these plays, including the personalities and their dispositions, and the conduct of the characters.'[43]

This technical pressure seems, as Voltaire was complaining, to be focused on the second word of the rhyme pair. If the first rhyme-word is essential to the meaning, the second, which may also, and ideally, be essential to the meaning, then has an additional necessity: sound. This constraint places 'Pasiphaé' firmly in the sound world. With respect to meaning, it could be pointed out that the rhyme which was most easily available to Racine at this moment is the rhyme 'fille-famille'. This rhyme is especially common in *Iphigénie*, and it is the closing rhyme of *Phèdre*. The 'subject' of this couplet could loosely be said to be Phèdre the daughter and her family. But it is not the referentiality of the words which is at issue here: it is their sound. The rhyme of 'Pasiphaé' stands in for the non-existent rhyme of 'Phèdre'. And, the periphrasis for the unrhymable name of Phèdre itself flirts with the unrhymable, has to be excused on this basis, and the crisis continues. What is being sought by this famous Alexandrine is a certain kind of sound, to rhyme the name of Phèdre, if only periphrastically. The result of this search has, in this one important way, left the project balanced on a precarious edge. Bremond called

First published 1999

Published for the Society for French Studies by the
European Humanities Research Centre
of the University of Oxford
47 Wellington Square
Oxford OX1 2JF

LEGENDA is the publications imprint of the
European Humanities Research Centre

Published 2017 by Routledge
2 Park Square, Milton Park, Abingdon, Oxon OX14 4RN
711 Third Avenue, New York, NY 10017, USA

Routledge is an imprint of the Taylor & Francis Group, an informa business

ISBN 13: 978-1-900755-14-6 (pbk)
ISSN 1466-8157

British Library Cataloguing in Publication Data
A CIP catalogue record for this book is available from the British Library

LEGENDA series designed by Cox Design Partnership, Witney, Oxon

Furetière says: 'Cadence, en termes de Poësie, signifie une certaine mesure de vers'. And lest we be still puzzled—how is this different from metre?—Furetière gives 'cadence' as 'la mesure égale que le cheval doit garder en tous ses mouvements, soit qu'il manie au galop, ou terre à terre, ou dans les airs, en telle sorte qu'un de ses temps n'embrasse pas plus de terrain que l'autre, & qu'il ait de la justesse dans tous ses mouvements'. The seventeenth-century French 'cadence', then, might translate into English as 'measured cadence', or 'steady beat'. Tragic language, in other words, must have a good beat, it must maintain a steady tempo. This accords well with what the Greek notion of *rhythmizein* is generally considered to have been: to regulate, to bring into measured time.[48] It has been recently translated into French as 'rythme'.[49]

Secondly, Racine translates the Greek *harmonian* with 'harmonie', while Vettori gives *harmoniam*. This would seem to be an unproblematic transmission of cognates. But a warning note is sounded when we discover that the recent French translation gives 'mélodie' at this point. Indeed, the ancient Greek understanding of the word seems to have included an understanding of the word as descriptive of the seven species of the octave, the Greek modes (Dorian, Lydian, Mixolydian, and so on).[50] So, Racine's translation, although it seems transparent, is not exactly a neutral gesture. And, were it to be argued that he had no leeway in the matter, that the available cognate imposed itself irresistibly, that argument would be complicated by Racine's third translation choice.

This spicy discourse, Aristotle writes, is, in the third place, characterized by *melos*. The Greek understanding of this term was that it referred to a song or tune, choral or lyric song, and melody generally.[51] Hence its recent translation into French as 'chant'.[52] For *melos*, however, Vettori gives 'metrum', which clearly refers to poetic rhythm and metre rather than to any melodic or tuneful aspect of language; and Racine follows Vettori, rendering *melos* as 'mesure', thus coming dangerously close to a redundancy with his initial 'cadence'. Indeed, for 'mesure', Furetière gives, 'se dit aussi des cadences & des temps qu'on doit observer en Poësie, à la danse & en Musique, pour les rendre agreables & regulieres. Les vers hexametres, pentamestres, Jambiques, Saphiques, sont de differentes mesures.' It is thus fairly clear that what Racine probably meant by 'mesure' is what we call metre in poetry. But what has become of the lost 'melos'?

It is important to understand that the Greek which Racine was reading at this point in his translation was 'metron'. But, further, Racine would have known that that word was unattested because Vettori's commentary explains this clearly and at length. Vettori simply emended the Greek text at this point on the basis of no textual evidence. The great Florentine humanist's reason for doing so is, as he states, 'that *melos* and *harmonia* mean the same' (57). He notes that 'learned and precise commentators have laboured greatly in order to explain this part; for they saw that if it was read in that way, many great difficulties arose. But when that error is indeed eliminated, everything is evident and clear' (57). 'It [the word *melos*] is therefore omitted, nor is it considered that this passage contains the words of the author, since he could not have been obscure or ambiguous' (58). The loss of *melos* as one of the condiments of tragic language, moreover, reinforces Vettori's opinion that song in the tragedy was limited to choral singing: 'It should be noticed that he himself calls the verses *metra* which are generated by the actors, and indeed all the parts of the tragedy, with the exception of those parts sung by the chorus, which are called *meloi*' (58).

What, then, is to be understood by Racine's following of Vettori on this point? With respect to transmission, the argument advanced long ago by René Bray is underlined: that the *Poetics* was the source of classical doctrine is an illusion. In fact, the text was known in France only through its Italian commentators, who deformed it. 'C'est sous le drapeau de l'aristotélisme que l'italianisme a pu pénétrer en France.'[53] But, more broadly, Racine's and Vettori's elimination of the explicit mention of song from the tragedy participates in a micro-logical way in a long history of the philosophical mistrust of music. Philosophical treatments of music beginning with Plato consider music to be a dangerous force which threatens fundamental social and political conventions. Music, from ancient times, has been construed as a path to moral ruin.[54] If Jacques Attali is correct, music has been considered dangerous, destructive and subversive because musical styles prophesy changes in social and political organization, changes which are profoundly threatening to the powers of the moment.[55] The discourse of tragedy, then, 'composé pour le plaisir', is already suspect, and 'melos' would have aggravated the problem.

Accordingly, what we have here is not so much a translation of Aristotle as a transmission of a peculiarly Racinian poetics as a reflection of Italian humanism. According to that poetics, tragedy and tragic language are to be considered separately. While tragedy is an imitation and a proper subject of the study of poetics, tragic language is a blurry instrumentality, something which one uses in order to make tragedy. The force of this formulation comes out clearly in the comparison of the three qualitites of that language in Greek as *rhuthmon*, *harmonian*, and *melos*, with Vettori's 'numerum et harmoniam et metrum', Racine's 'cadence, harmonie et mesure', and their recent translation as 'rythme, mélodie et chant'. Tempo, metre, and harmony characterize tragic language for Racine. What has been lost in the translation is the unequivocal reference to sounding music: *melos*. Replaced by another reference to number, and at the cost of a certain redundancy, *melos* is lost to the language of tragedy for Racine.

And yet—the stage of explicitly musical language, the contemporary opera of Lully and Quinault, bodies forth a structure which confirms the articulation which we have just seen to be operative between the tragedy and its own language. How are we to understand that stage's relationship to its own language? This articulation thematized itself in the operatic prologue, and we may read the prologue to *Atys* of Lully and Quinault, the court opera produced immediately prior to *Phèdre*, in order to see this thematization in action.[56]

The genre which we call 'opera' called itself, on its title pages, 'tragédie' or sometimes 'tragédie mise en musique', and the enormous theoretical foundations and implications of this terminological identity have recently been the subject of important scholarly work.[57] And the recently renewed interest in word–music relationships on the French seventeenth-century stage,[58] along with the re-evaluation of the opera of Lully and Quinault,[59] has been productive of a re-reading of the operatic prologue. Once generally dismissed as 'purely panegyric and decorative',[60] 'transparent allegorical tales [...] in which the "official history" of Louis XIV's reign unfolded',[61] 'une courte pièce détachée qui n'a, en général, pour objet que l'éloge du roi',[62] the operatic prologue, as is now recognized, may take as its project not only encomium but also the announcement of its own theoretical bases.[63] This is particularly striking in the case of the prologue to *Atys*.

The Prologue begins with the announcement by the figure of Time that he has lost control of historical memory. The effect of the present hero has been practically to erase the names which Time has respected:

En vain j'ay respecté la celebre memoire
　　Des heros des siècles passez;
C'est en vain que leur nom si fameux dans l'Histoire,
Du sort des noms communs ont esté dispensez:
Nous voyons un heros dont la brillante gloire
　　Les a presque tous effacez. (1–6)

There follows the Chorus of Hours which confirms the subjugation of time, 'chaque jour, chaque instant' (10), to the task of adding glory to his name. The Prologue then continues with two *entrées de ballet*: the first, 'La déesse Flore conduite par un des Zephirs, [...] avec une troupe de nymphes, qui portent divers ornements de fleurs' (55); and the second, 'Melpomene, qui est la muse qui preside à la tragedie, [...] accompagnée d'une troupe de heros' (57). Of all the references circulating through this beginning of the opera, this moment of intra-representational reference is the most important structurally. What does it mean for a genre which calls itself not 'opéra' but rather 'tragédie' to stage the appearance of itself? And, working backwards, if the *tragédie* represents the entrance of its own muse, then who or what was the deceptively innocent Flore?

Flore is firstly another element within the representation which does not obey Time. The conceit of the *livret* is that Flore appears out of season:

Le froid cruel regne encore;
Tout est glacé dans les champs,
D'où vient que Flore
Devance le printemps? (17–20)

Flore is thus aligned with the 'heros' whose effect has been to defeat historical memory. Flore represents this effect in the field of the allegorical. She is a moment of allegory gone wrong, for Time, who has already lost control of heroic reputation, here loses control of nature. Seeing Flore and her troupe of flowers appear in January, he can only ask, 'Quel dieu les fait renaistre/ Lorsque l'hyver les fait mourir?' (15–16). As allegory, Flore points to the re-writing of the allegorical which is being undertaken by the Prologue. She has become unmoored from the springtime, and from Time itself, and is now free for other signifying tasks.

The figure of Flore is taken, as are the character of Atys and the subject of the opera, from Ovid's *Fasti* (v. 183–378). While Quinault's Flore has as her project, we might say, the escaping of allegorical constraint, Ovid's goddess has a darker story to tell. Firstly, the Zéphir who accompanies Flore in the Prologue has, in Ovid, raped Flora in the springtime of the year and forced her to marry him. A limited, specific example of the dark Ovidian undertone to the Prologue would thus be Zéphir's *air*, 'Le printemps quelquefois est moins doux qu'il ne semble,/ Il fait trop payer ses beaux jours' (35–6).

Secondly, Ovid's Flora is the agent of the metamorphosis of the blood of dead heroes into flowers. This is true not only for the blood of Hyacinthus, Crocus, and Narcissus, but also for the blood spilled by the self-castration of Atys, which was turned into violets.[64] In Quinault's text, this transformative power is not exactly absent; rather, it goes underground and emerges in the last act as the metamorphosis of Atys into a pine tree by the goddess Cybèle. At this moment in the final act, there is an analogical entrée of Flore:

> Atys, au printemps de son âge,
> Perit comme une fleur
> Qu'un soudain orage
> Renverse et ravage. (1059–62)

The rape of Flora by a wind in the springtime, which had been shut out of the Prologue, here enters with a vengeance. Atys himself is now the flower ('une fleur') whom a wind ('un soudain orage') rapes ('renverse et ravage') in the springtime ('au printemps de son âge'). But in this final act, this analogy substitutes for the scene of self-castration, which is itself denied by Quinault's text. In Quinault, far from becoming a eunuch priest, Atys murders the nymph Sangaride, kills himself, and becomes a pine tree. From these two points of comparison between Quinault's Flore and Ovid's Flora, the extent of Quinault's re-writing begins to become apparent. 'Flore', and the becoming-Flore of Atys, is the index to the difference with respect to the tragic action between the received ancient text and the early modern one.

The question of Flore's identity becomes acute with the appearance on the stage of Melpomene, the tragic muse. She is accompanied by a troupe of her own, a retinue of ancient heroes ready to restage in pantomime their legendary struggles. Her *récit* is preceded by its own prelude, casting the allegory of Time and Flore into a kind of pre-stage, a mere preparation for the real event of this *tragédie*, which is the appearance of Tragedy. Indeed, Melpomene claims the stage as her own:

Que l'agrement rustique
De Flore & de ses jeux,
Cede à l'appareil magnifique
De la Muse tragique,
Et de ses spectacles pompeux. (46–50)

By 'spectacles pompeux', what Melpomene means is exactly the kind of representation that Time had begun the Prologue by declaring to be impossible. Melpomene is accompanied onto the stage by a retinue of ancient heroes, Hercules, Anteus, Castor and Pollux, and so on. They now 'recommencent leurs anciennes querelles' (58). The agents of the tragic muse thus operate in a theoretical vacuum. Time himself has declared them to be unrepresentable. 'La celebre memoire/ Des heros des siècles passez' has been practically erased. The nature of this erasure, however, is not visual but rather auditory: the heroes of tragedy have been silenced, staging their ancient quarrels as a militaristic ballet. What they lack, that is, is language, 'un discours, un style, composé pour le plaisir'.

It is accordingly no surprise that the take-over of the stage ordered by Melpomene is unsuccessful: Cybèle, the controlling goddess of the tragedy which will follow the Prologue, sends Iris to 'accorder Melpomene et Flore' (58). 'Cybele veut que Flore aujourd'huy vous seconde,/ Il faut que les plaisirs viennent de toutes parts' (51–2). Representation then obeys what it is about to represent, and 'la suite de Melpomene s'accorde avec la suite de Flore' (58).

Flore is thus a fundamentally structural figure. The content of the tragic muse's spectacles, the ancient struggles of legendary heroes, has been declared erased, and her heroes, incapable of singing, can only ever dance. This is the situation which causes the opera to open itself up to Flore. She is that surplus agency which joins with the *tragédie* to make the genre which insisted upon itself as *tragédie*. This juncture is not to be understood as a *Gesamtkunstwerk*. What is being proposed in the articulation accomplished by the Prologue is not a concept of the opera as a union of the arts, but rather a concept of opera as a joining of tragedy and Flore. Flore is the opera's discourse; she is what enables it to sing. She is its pleasure, that without which the tragedy would be but pantomime. Not the tragic muse, Flore yet is that without which the tragic muse is strictly unstageable. Indeed, she is what makes this tragedy itself: French, not Latin, and not Greek. The operatic Flore relates to Melpomene exactly as Racine's 'style composé pour le plaisir' relates to his 'imitation grave et complète'. Flore is tragic language made visible.

So, something which has been stamped out of tragic language by Racine, and which seems to occupy for both the operatic stage and the *Poetics* of Aristotle the position of the supplemental agency of pleasure, a musical tragic language, has nevertheless been historically considered to be the primary feature of Racine's tragedy, and even to be that tragedy itself. What, we might well wonder, has happened?

It would seem that the very force with which the music of tragic language was denied by Racine caused that music not only to re-enter the stage of the tragedy, but also to stage a takeover, and that it is that takeover which has been heard from that day to this. This experience of hearing has received varying formulations, but, silent or sounding, it is no generalized hallucination. Our famous Alexandrine, 'La fille de Minos et de Pasiphaé', will illustrate this dynamic.

If the operatic prologue indeed displays and promotes its own procedural parameters, the first scene of *Phèdre* may be said to do the same. There, virtuosity in language is displayed in the technique of the 'rime-sécurité', the procedure in which the power of suggestion moves through the requirement of the end-rhyme. The name of Phèdre, unrhymable, is unavailable to this procedure. Unavailable as well is the name which comes to replace the name of Phèdre, that of her mother, Pasiphaé, whose borderline unrhymability serves to point up the problem. The kernel of the problem is the syllable beginning with the Greek *phi*, and that syllable's referential meaning is fundamentally, and in an originary sense, visual. That is, the naming procedure of both Pasiphae and Phaedre was like that of racehorses: as descendants of the sun, their names both refer to the quality of light. 'Phaedre' means 'the beaming one', and 'Pasiphae' means literally 'for all (pasi) the one who shines (phae)', and so, perhaps, 'the one who shines on everything'.[65]

In the most basic sense, then, the project of the first scene of *Phèdre* might be said to be that of making the visual not just sound, but more precisely of making it sing: to cause the name of Phèdre to rhyme, to accord with another bit of the sound-world, to make this name harmonize with something else. It is, as I have argued, a failed project. And what has over the years been heard as the musicality of Racinian language can be nothing other than this spectacular failure, this approximation of singing light. In this sense, the *tragédie* and the *tragédie mise en musique* are secret sharers. They share the same constraints and conceptualization of tragic language, but that language is actualized differently. The *tragédie mise en musique* ushers on to the stage the musicality of its language, frolics about with it, and opens itself up to the sound of music. But the *tragédie* causes its own musicality to exist in a gap, a kind of meta-hiatus between sound and sense which acute listeners have always heard, and which the theory of its own language, filtered through Florentine humanism, has denied.

Is this going too far? In historical terms, we could note that one of the great teacher Vettori's greatest pupils was Girolomo Mei, 'mentor to the Florentine Camerata', whose project was to recreate the musical qualities of ancient Greek, and who presided over the invention of the genre which later came to be known as opera.[66] And any further consideration of this matter would have to contend with the probability that, when he engaged himself to write an opera, the one name which Racine would have caused to be sung was that of the title character, Phaeton, whose name is the gerund of the Greek verb, 'to shine'.[67] To cause the shining to sing: the project failed once again, and failed specifically to the master of the tragic stage. For those geniuses of the opera, Lully and Quinault, presented as their opera for the 1683 season, *Phaéton*.

It is a kind of pre-nostalgia, a nostalgia-in-advance, this musicality of Racinian language. It is an echo only, of some unknown something, perhaps irretrievably lost. All that we can know further of the situation is that, after *Phaéton*, Racine gave up this particular form of pursuing the project, turned away from the Greeks and the Greek language, and, by the time that Moreau's 'Prélude pour la Piété qui descend du Ciel' sounded the beginning of *Esther*,[68] his hunt for this missing something had led him both far afield, and, to a certain extent, home again. *Phèdre* marks the perihelion of Racine's tragic language. It is this orbit which she describes, and this song which she sings.

Notes to chapter 1

1. 'From a reading of most criticism [...] one would imagine that what really matters is poetry (in the narrow sense) or psychology or ideas.' H. T. Barnwell, *The Tragic Drama of Corneille and Racine. An Old Parallel Revisited* (Oxford: Clarendon Press, 1982), 94.

2. Louis Racine, 'Mémoires sur la vie et les ouvrages de Jean Racine', in *Racine. Œuvres complètes*, ed. Raymond Picard (Paris: Gallimard (Bibliothèque de la Pléiade), 1950), i. 60.
3. Antoine Furetière, *Le Dictionnaire universel* (1690) (Paris: SNL-Le Robert, 1978).
4. Pier Vettori (ed.), *Commentarii in primum librum Aristotles De Arte poetarum*, 2nd edn. (In Officina Juntarum: Bernardi Filiorum, 1573), 57.
5. Roselyne Dupont-Roc and Jean Lallot (trans.), *Aristote. La Poétique* (Paris: Seuil, 1980), 53.
6. *Oxford Latin Dictionary*, 1982 edn.
7. Alain Viala, *Racine. La Stratégie du caméléon* (Paris: Seghers, 1990), 176.
8. Lytton Strachey, 'Racine' (1908), *Books and Characters French and English* (New York: Harcourt, Brace, 1922), 6.
9. Paul Pellisson Fontanier and l'abbé d'Olivet, *Histoire de l'Académie française*, 2 vols. (Paris: Didier, 1858), ii. 325–47.
10. See Dominique Muller, 'Aspects de la déclamation dans le récitatif de Jean-Baptiste Lully', *Forum musicologicum* 2 (1980), 132–51.
11. Jean Laurent Le Cerf de la Viéville, *Comparaison de la musique italienne et de la musique française* (1705) (Geneva: Minkoff, 1972), 108.
12. Emile Mas, *La Champmeslé* (Paris: Félix Alcan, 1932), 23–34.
13. L. Aimé-Martin (ed.), 'Préface de la première édition publiée en 1820', *Œuvres complètes de J. Racine avec les notes de tous les commentateurs*, 5th edn. (Paris: Lefèvre et Furne, 1844), pp. xii-xiii.
14. Denis Diderot, *Paradoxe sur le comédien* (Paris: Flammarion, 1981), 127.
15. La Harpe, *Cours de littérature ancienne et moderne* (Paris: Dupont, 1826), viii. 120–1.
16. Alfred de Musset, *Œuvres complètes* (Paris: Seuil, 1963), 898.
17. Gonzague Truc, 'La "nouveauté" dans la langue de Racine', *Revue d'histoire littéraire de la France* 22 (1915), 132–46.
18. 'Partout où la monarchie se reproduira, Racine trouvera des partisans.' *Racine et Shakespeare*, 285. Racine is nevertheless claimed by Claudel for the company of the victims of political oppression, with reference to the warrant issued for his arrest by the secret police at the time of the 'Affaire des Poisons'. *Conversation sur Jean Racine* (Paris: Gallimard, 1956), 14.
19. Lytton Strachey, *Books and Characters French and English* (New York: Harcourt, Brace, 1922), 19.
20. Quoted in Arthur Gold and Robert Fizdale, *The Divine Sarah. A Life of Sarah Bernhardt* (New York: Alfred Knopf, 1991), 151.
21. Henri Bremond, *Racine et Valéry. Notes sur l'initiation poétique* (Paris: Grasset, 1931).
22. A. C. Bradley, *Oxford Lectures on Poetry* (London: Macmillan, 1909).
23. Bremond, *Racine et Valéry*, p. x.
24. Henri Bremond, *La Poésie pure* (Paris: Grasset, 1926), 15.
25. Bremond, *La Poésie pure*, 31–8.
26. 1916–32. Paris: Armand Colin, 1967.
27. Erich Auerbach, 'Figura', in *Scenes from the Drama of European Literature* (Minneapolis, University of Minnesota Press, 1984), 11–76.
28. Louis Marin, *Le Portrait du roi* (Paris: Minuit, 1981). See also my 'Medea, Poison, and the Epistemology of Error in *Phèdre*', *MLR* (forthcoming, 1999).

29. Proust, of whom Souday was also fiercely critical, once referred to him as 'ce méchant' (letter of 9 or 10 Dec. 1913 to André Beaunier, in *Correspondance*, ed. Philip Kolb [Paris: Plon, 1984], xii. 376), and he formulated the puzzling nature of Souday's criticism in a letter to Souday himself: 'On pourrait dire, il me semble, que vous ne vous prêtez pas à la transfiguration voulue par l'auteur, que vous mettez l'œuvre d'art (et c'est d'autant plus bizarre que vous avez une prédilection esthétique très sûre) sur le même plan que la vie commune' (letter of 15 Nov. 1920 (xix. 594–5)).
30. André Malraux, *Les Voix du silence* (Paris: Gallimard, 1951), 333.
31. Gonzague Truc, *Jean Racine: l'œuvre, l'artiste, l'homme et le temps* (Paris: Garnier, 1926).
32. Paul Valéry, 'Discours sur Henri Bremond', in *Œuvres* (Paris: Gallimard, 1957), i. 763–9.
33. Blaise Pascal, *Pensées*, in *Œuvres complètes* (Paris: Seuil, 1963), no. 265.
34. 'Rime', says Furetière, 'signifie quelquefois les vers & la Poësie même.' On the theory of rhyme, see Arthur Melville Clark and Harold Whitehall, 'Rhyme', *Princeton Encyclopedia of Poetry and Poetics*; Marjorie Perloff, *Rhyme and Meaning in the Poetry of Yeats* (The Hague and Paris: Mouton, 1970), 43–99. On rhyme in French poetry, see Clive Scott, *French Verse-art: A Study* (Cambridge: Cambridge University Press, 1980); Clive Scott, *The Riches of Rhyme* (Oxford: Clarendon Press, 1988); W. D. Howarth, 'Some Thoughts on the Function of Rhyme in French Classical Tragedy', in *The Equilibrium of Wit. Essays for Odette de Mourges*, ed. Peter Bayley and Dorothy Gabe Coleman (Lexington: French Forum, 1982), 150–65.
35. Boileau's reference is to the epic poem, 'Childebrand ou les Sarrasins chassés de France', first published in 1667, by Jacques Carel de Sainte-Garde. In 1679, a revised version of the poem appeared, with the hero's name changed to Charles Martel. Charles-H. Boudhors, *Nicolas Boileau-Despréaux. Epîtres, Art Poétique, Lutrin* (Paris: Belles-Lettres, 1952), 229.
36. Théodore de Banville, *Petit traité de versification française*, in *Œuvres* (1871) (Geneva: Slatkine, 1972), viii. 80.
37. Jacques-Gabriel Cahen, *Le Vocabulaire de Racine* (1946) (Geneva: Slatkine, 1970), 171.
38. Cahen, *Le Vocabulaire de Racine*, 175.
39. One recent rhyme dictionary lists no fewer than 19 rhymes on 'èdre', including 'icosaèdre' and 'mourvèdre' (Armel Louis, *Dictionnaire des rimes et assonances* (Paris: Les Usuels, 1997)); the only one which apears in the Racinian vocabulary, however, is 'cèdre', found only once (*Esther*, iii. 9. 1209), and never rhymed. Bryant C. Freeman and Alan Batson, *Concordance du théâtre et des poésies de Jean Racine* (Ithaca: Cornell University Press, 1968), i. 172. The difficulty of this rhyme was noticed in Paul Scarron, 'La Foire Saint Germain': 'Nous boirons de l'aigre de cedre/ Mais comment diable ferons-nous/ Pour trouver une rime en edre?' (230–2). *Poésies diverses*, ed. Maurice Cauchie (Paris: Didier, 1947), i. 20.
40. Louis Racine, 'Remarques sur les tragédies de Jean Racine' (1752), in *Œuvres complètes* (1808) (Geneva: Slatkine, 1969), vi. 161.
41. 'When the vowel which determines rime is not followed by a consonant, rime and assonance are one and the same thing: loi, roi.' L. E. Kastner, *A History of French Versification* (Oxford: Clarendon Press, 1903), 40.

42. 'Préface de l'édition [d'*Œdipe*] de 1730', in *Œuvres complètes de Voltaire*, nouvelle édition, *Théâtre* (Paris: Garnier, 1877), i. 41. This quotation is from the fifth of seven 'Lettres écrites en 1719'.
43. 'Die Eigenschaft des Alexandriners, sich in zwei gleiche Hälften zu trennen, und die Natur des Reims, aus zwei Alexandrinern ein Couplet zu machen, bestimmen nicht bloss die ganze Sprache, sie bestimmen auch den ganzen inneren Geist dieser Stücke, die Charaktere, die Gesinnungen, das Betragen der Personen.' Quoted in Dieter Steland, 'Racines *Phèdre* in den Übersetzungen von Friedrich Schiller und Simon Werle', *Zeitschrift für französische Sprache und Literatur* 102 (1992), 65.
44. Eugène Vinaver (ed.), *Racine. Principes de la tragédie en marge de la poétique d'Aristote* (Manchester and Paris: Manchester University Press and Nizet, 1978), 5.
45. Paul Mesnard (ed.), *Œuvres de Jean Racine* (Paris: Hachette, 1865), v. 432–3.
46. For the Greek text, as well as a recent translation, I refer to Dupont-Roc and Lallot.
47. See Vinaver, cited above, and Roy C. Knight, *Racine et la Grèce* (Paris: Nizet, 1974), 195–206.
48. Solon Michaelides, *The Music of Ancient Greece. An Encyclopedia* (London: Faber and Faber, 1978), s.v. 'rhythmos'.
49. Dupont-Roc and Lallot, 53.
50. Michaelides, *The Music of Ancient Greece*, s.v. 'harmonia'.
51. Michaelides, *The Music of Ancient Greece*, s.v. 'melos'.
52. Dupont-Roc and Lallot, 53.
53. René Bray, *La Formation de la doctrine classique en France* (Paris: Hachette, 1927), 49.
54. See Mladen Dolar, 'The Object Voice', in *Gaze and Voice as Love Objects*, ed. Renata Salecl and Slavoj Žižek (Durham and London: Duke University Press, 1996), 7–31.
55. Jacques Attali, *Noise. The Political Economy of Music*, trans. Brian Massumi (Minneapolis: University of Minnesota Press, 1985).
56. On Lully and Quinault, see Etienne Gros, *Philippe Quinault. Sa vie et son œuvre* (Paris: Champion, 1926); Cuthbert Girdlestone, *La Tragédie en musique (1673–1750) considérée comme genre littéraire* (Geneva: Droz, 1972); Manuel Couvreur, *Jean-Baptiste Lully. Musique et dramaturgie au service du Prince* (n.p.: Marc Volkar Editeur, 1992); Philippe Beaussant, *Lully, ou le musicien du soleil* (Paris: Gallimard, 1992); Emmanuel Haymann, *Lulli* (Paris: Flammarion, 1991).
57. Catherine Kintzler, *Poétique de l'opéra français de Corneille à Rousseau* (Paris: Minerve, 1991).
58. See Kintzler; Nicolas Cronk, 'Molière-Charpentier's *Le Malade Poétique imaginaire*: the First *Opéra-comique*', *Forum for Modern Language Studies* 29 (1993), 216–31; Nicolas Cronk, 'The Play of Words and Music in Molière-Charpentier's *Le Malade imaginaire*', *French Studies* 47 (1993), 6–19.
59. Jérôme de la Gorce and Herbert Schneider (eds.), *Jean-Baptiste Lully. Actes du colloque Saint-Germain-en-Laye/Heidelberg 1987* (Laaber: Laaber-Verlag, 1990); John Hajdu Heyer (ed.), *Jean-Baptiste Lully and the Music of the French Baroque: Essays in Honor of James R. Anthony* (Cambridge: Cambridge University Press, 1989); William Brooks, 'Seventeenth-Century Culture: Quinault and Lully

Resurgent', *French Studies Bulletin*, 47 (1993), 17–19. See also Couvreur, *Jean-Baptiste Lully*; Beaussant, *Lully*; Haymann, *Lulli*, cited above.

60. James R. Anthony, *French Baroque Music from Beaujoyeulx to Rameau* (New York: Norton, 1974), 71.

61. Robert M. Isherwood, *Music in the Service of the King: France in the Seventeenth Century* (Ithaca and London: Cornell University Press, 1973), 208.

62. Etienne Gros, *Philippe Quinault*, 523.

63. Stephane Bassinet (ed.), *Philippe Quinault. Atys. Edition critique* (Geneva: Droz, 1992), 31. All further references are to this edition.

64. v. 227. See Henri Le Bonniec (trans.), *Les Fastes* (Bologna: Pàtron, 1970), 126 n. 56.

65. Frederick Ahl (trans.), *Seneca. Three Tragedies* (Ithaca and London: Cornell University Press, 1986), 173–4.

66. Lidia Caciolli, 'Giovanni da Falgano fra Pier Vettori e la Camarata de'Bardi', *Rinascimento* 31 (1991), 309–24 (318). On Mei, see Claude Palisca, 'Mentor to the Florentine Camerata', *Musical Quarterly* 40 (1954), 1–20.

67. *Oxford English Dictionary*, 1989 edn. On Racine's opera project, see my 'Boileau and the Sound of Satire', *Forum for Modern Language Studies* 31 (1995), 128–39.

68. Jean-Baptiste Moreau, *Chœurs de la tragédie d'Esther avec la musique composée par J. B. Moreau, Maistre de Musique du Roi* (Paris: Thierry, Barbin et Ballard, 1689).

CHAPTER 2

Design
Death of Hippolytus

Since the appearance in 1954 of Jean Starobinski's influential essay on 'Racine et la poétique du regard', questions of seeing and being seen, problems of light and darkness, shadow and clarity, have been considered central to the poetics of Racinian tragedy.[1] In part a reaction against the discourse of the 'musicality' of Racinian language which we have just been looking into, Starobinski's essay is much concerned with what might be called the gaze of desire. Racine's letter of 24 November 1661 from Uzès, in which he watches women watching fireworks, while his own attention is watched by the policing gaze of 'un R. Père de ce chapitre', provides the structure of 'le regard regardé', which resurfaces in the visions of Pyrrhus, Néron and Phèdre. What is interesting about Starobinski's analysis is its insistence upon the failure of the desiring gaze: ever an imperfect grasp of the desired object, it is characterized by a blind spot or shadow, and productive of a character complex which gives the impression of truth precisely because it is never entirely visible. Starobinski speaks of a 'battement sémantique' of the verb 'voir', and he replays, with all of the profound insight of the second Geneva School, the seventeenth-century battle of the ears and the eyes. If the power of the gaze is indeed contained within the poetic line, creating a horizon at which the word vanishes, then that word has caused there to come into being that which it would seem to exclude: silence (77).

For all of its great beauty, however, Starobinski's essay places enormous weight upon the assumption that the act of seeing is trans-temporal. Yet there is another kind of question which can perhaps be asked. If the tragedy for Racine was quite different from that which we would assume it to be, if it was not congruent with the collection of Alexandrines which materially constitute it, then it would seem that caution, at least, is advisable with respect to 'voir'. Firstly, there is not just one, uniformly analysable, Racinian gaze. While Starobinski was concerned with the structure of the desiring gaze, there is another function of vision in *Phèdre*, and it is the function which characterizes the rhetorical figure of 'setting the thing before the eyes', the hypotyposis, and the related figure of speech, enargeia, which 'makes us seem not so much to narrate as to bring to life the actual scene'.[2] The project of Phèdre's 'ou tel que je vous voi' (ii. 5. 640), which responds well to an analysis of the desiring gaze which is constituted by its very failure to seize its object, is quite distinct from that of Théramène's 'j'ai vu' (v. 6. 1547). The importance of the latter, indeed its determining status for the question of vision in *Phèdre*, is suggested by the productivity of recent readings which treat the entire tragedy as an example of enargeia.[3]

Secondly, the question would arise of the historicity of the Racinian gaze. The choice of 'le regard' as an umbrella term, and its usual translation into English as 'the gaze', references the Lacanian gaze, one whose subject both constitutes and is constituted by the object of vision.[4] Is this a valid, or a particularly helpful or pertinent, dynamic from within which to see the tragedy? The modalities of the constitution of the subject are a problem which concerns us, and has concerned us since Freud, very much. But it is not, I would argue, a central or necessary concern of a tragedy writer's vision in the French seventeenth century. That concern would have been with the tragic action. 'Action' should be understood as being a structure characterized by a vision gap, in much the same way as is the desiring gaze, but this is a gap which is constitutive not of the post-Renaissance individual or of any transcendent subject, but rather of the imitation which is the tragedy. It is a structure, further, contemporary with Racinian tragedy, and it has everything to do with the relationship between words and images on the tragic stage.

When the abbé d'Aubignac, in one of the century's most important theoretical statements on the stage, declares that 'Parler, c'est agir',[5] he names a structure which has given rise to a book-length analysis,[6] and one which formulates precisely the mutually dependent status of word and action on the stage. 'En un mot, les Discours ne sont au Theatre que les accessoires de l'Action, quoy que toute la Tragédie, dans la Representation ne consiste qu'en Discours' (282–3). So, the play consists entirely of language, yet language is but an accessory. The materiality of the play, its being for the ear, yet creates through itself something beyond itself, action. It is difficult to understand what exactly d'Aubignac might be referring to here, and Hawcroft has shown that the conceptual field of 'action' in the seventeenth century was multi-layered.[7] The theorists generally insisted upon a distinction between action and plot, or 'la fable': 'L'action est l'œuvre du héros, la fable celle du poète', as René Bray, summarizing Mambrun, long ago reminded us.[8] Action is what the tragedy imitates: in Racine's translation of the problematic definition, 'la tragédie est donc l'imitation d'une action grave et complète'. But another way in which the term 'action' was understood came close to being identical with the visual component of the tragedy. This notion of action as 'things done visibly' (Hawcroft, 17) is the lowest common denominator of drama. It is shared with staged representations, film, and acting of all kinds. So it is not the specificity of this action itself upon which I will be insisting here, but rather the specificity of the structure into which this visual component fits. D'Aubignac's notion of 'agir' can be applied indifferently to tragedies either ancient or modern. He gives as examples of it scenes from Seneca and Corneille. But what is interesting and specific about the structure revealed by d'Aubignac's 'parler, c'est agir' is its correspondence to the structure of one particular kind of early modern gaze. D'Aubignac prefaces his remarks upon the curious visual productivity of verse with an insistence upon the visual constitution of the play: 'Ceux-là méme qui s'y trouvent presens s'appellent Spectateurs ou Regardans, et non pas Auditeurs' (282). Again, he states this problematic structure, this time explicitly in terms of vision: 'On trouvera que les Actions ne sont que dans l'imagination du Spectateur, à qui le Poëte par adresse les fait concevoir comme visibles, et cependant qu'il n'y a rien de sensible que le discours' (283). We have indeed reached here the place which Starobinski called the horizon at which the word vanishes, and what is created beyond this horizon is indeed silence, but, for the seventeenth century, that silence had substance. It was an image. This image stands in that silent place beyond discourse: created by it, yet radically not of it. This mutually dependent, yet materially independent relationship of word and image is constitutive not primarily of the subject, but rather of the imitation which is the tragedy. When we speak of 'the gaze', for the seventeenth century, we speak necessarily not just of action, in reference to d'Aubignac, but more precisely of something like this action's technical procedure, that is, interaction, an interactivity of word and image which is both interdependent and mutually exclusive. What Starobinski called 'le regard', then, may be said in the theoretical sense not to have been emphasized by the seventeenth century, pertinent as it may be for our own encounters with subjectivity. It participates in a chronology of gazes. This is the general response to the question of the historicity of the Racinian gaze. When we ask the question, 'What gaze?', 'Whose gaze?', and do not assume a stable trans-temporality called 'the gaze', the inquiry lights out in a different direction: towards the theatre rather than towards the self.

This textually based gaze could be called a kind of national vision which Racine and his contemporaries inherited from Renaissance humanism. In French culture from the sixteenth century, there was a habit of thinking about texts in visual terms, and about pictures in literary terms, which stands quite apart from the neo-Platonist formulation of the word-image relation as 'Ut pictura poesis'.[9] Whereas the neo-Platonist vision expected meaning to be immanent in the image, to be bodied forth as a function of the artist's intuiting of the universal form in the sensible object,[10] an alternative, and opposed, model for the fixing of meaning in the image relied upon interaction, either the interaction of word and image, or the interaction of a figure and objects in a pictorial composition which gloss it.[11] This latter procedure for seeing images and fixing their meaning, the procedure which 'broke the neo-Platonic spell' (Boas, 27), can broadly be called emblematic.

The emblem was the text-image form which historically seems to have borne most of the weight of the long conceptual transition from the certainty of medieval allegory to the indeterminacy of Romantic metaphor.[12] Emerging as a form in the early sixteenth century, the emblem rapidly became a pan-European phenomenon, and has been of interest not only to scholars of emblematic forms strictly defined, such as the emblem and device, but also to those interested in the characteristic text-image combinations of public monuments, the Trauerspiel, fables, machine plays and the novel.[13] In France around 1620 there began a process of definition, collection, and categorization of emblems and devices which reached its peak between 1650 and 1670 and was substantially complete by about 1685.[14] This project was carried out mainly by Jesuits, among the most prominent of whom were the most important iconographic historian of the seventeenth century, Claude-François Menestrier, and the grammarian and language theorist, Dominique Bouhours. As a publication venture, the production of emblems continued throughout the seventeenth century, with a re-edition of Ripa's *Iconology* appearing in Paris in the year of *Phèdre*'s première.[15]

Emblematics should be understood as a process rather than only as a form. It was a way of thinking about the combination of words and images, an attitude towards visual and literary art. An emblematic structure sets itself the problem of working out the reciprocal impact of picture and words, and that impact, distinguishing the emblem from contemporary word-image constructions such as the device, was usually held to be moral. Also, the emblem, like the tragedy, had a 'corps', which all theorists agree is the visual component of the emblem (Russell, 40). But the 'âme' of the emblem is not necessarily the words. Rather, as Menestrier claims in the 1662 *Art des emblemes*, the emblem's soul is its meaning, a moral lesson, and its words are the interpreters, the translators, of this meaning.[16] There clearly existed in the French seventeenth century not just an emblematic 'mechanics of reading' (Russell, 22), but also something like a generalized emblematic vision. It was possible for Menestrier to declare that 'les inventions des Poëtes sont presque toutes emblematiques'; and, in the 1684 *Art des emblemes*, a vast summary of the history, techniques and theory of the form, he claimed that 'L'Art des Emblêmes n'est plus à present que l'Art de peindre les moeurs et de mettre en images les operations de la nature pour l'instruction des hommes' (3).

None of this, however, will necessarily support any assertion that Racine shared this generalized vision. His best-known comment on an emblematic form relates to the removal of a 'nasty rat' from his family coat of arms.[17] Nevertheless, Margaret McGowan has argued for a conceptual continuity between Racine and Menestrier with respect to theatrical language;[18] Boileau himself theorized the inscriptions for the paintings of Le Brun in the Grande Galerie of Versailles as 'emblesmes heroïques';[19] and Racine probably collaborated in the composition of the inscriptions intended to replace those of Charpentier (Boudhors, 326–7). What is perhaps more important than these kinds of associational connections in arguing for Racine's sharing of the emblematic vision, however, are broad issues relating to the language and the purpose of the tragedy. That is, in the corps–âme structure of the emblem, the theorists' formulation of the words as simply the translators, a passage through from image to the soul of the emblem's moral meaning, may well be congruent with the status of the tragedy's language as 'figure', in the

Pascalian sense which I discussed in Chapter 1, as well as with d'Aubignac's formulation of tragic discourse as constituting action yet being at the same time but an accessory to the action itself. And the emblematic is one register, if not the only one, in which Racine's insistence in the Préface upon *Phèdre*'s instructiveness sounds. The theatre is a school, according to Racine, and instructing the spectators, he concludes, is 'la véritable intention de la tragédie'. Racine's tragedy thus shares two tremendously important conceptual structures with the emblem: the status of its word, and its ethical stance.

What we might call the 'emblematic gaze', then, is the one whose medium is productive of that which defines its own horizon: at the 'horizon at which the word vanishes', there is the visual image; and at the horizon at which they both vanish is the meaningfulness of the combination, the moral lesson, the soul, which is produced by the word and the image together but which is equivalent to neither one. There is certainly, following Starobinski, a poetics of the Racinian gaze, but this gaze functions within an emblematics as well.

The historical moment which found Racine at the height of his Parisian stage career was also the moment of a bitter contest in the Académie royale de peinture et de sculpture over the question of how the visual image should be conceptualized. This contest offers a second, more narrowly focused, answer to the question of the historicity of the Racinian gaze, and it finds an expression in Racine's own formulation of the technique of his moral instructiveness, from *Phèdre*'s Préface: 'Le vice y est peint partout avec des couleurs qui en font connaître et haïr la difformité.' This contest for the soul of painting is never an explicit reference for the Racinian text. But its stakes—the claims of Aristotelianism, the status of discourse, and the general project of visibility—are the stakes of the tragedy.

Just when the art of painting seemed to have acquired and consolidated its academic dignity as a theoretical and intellectual activity, the old Italian controversy which opposed Tuscan *disegno* to Lombard *colore* broke out again in the Academy and in the writing of the amateur who was to become the most important writer on art in France before Diderot, Roger de Piles.[20] The Académie royale de peinture et de sculpture had been founded in 1648, at a time when French painters were mainly unlettered, and painting in France was still considered to be a mercenary trade, subject to annual fees.[21] At a rapid pace, the Academy had centralized and increasingly come to control both the theory and practice of painting, consolidating and articulating the theoretical premisses which served to support the reigning political and religious orthodoxies, and, not incidentally, its own existence.[22] The emphasis of the theoretical project of the early Academy was that painting and literature were connected. Painting had a discursive rationality, a pedagogics, and a painting demanded to be read, not simply looked at. Painters, it was claimed, were intellectuals, and painting was a mental activity, not a work of the hand. In the words of the great spokesman of the early Academy, Félibien: 'Il est donc vray qu'il y a un Art tout particulier qui est détaché de la matiere et de la main de l'Artisan, par lequel il doit d'abord former ses Tableaux dans son esprit, et sans quoy un Peintre ne peut faire avec le pinceau seul un ouvrage parfait, n'estant pas de cét Art comme de ceux où l'industrie et l'adresse de la main suffisent pour donner de la beauté.'[23] Further, the locus of this idea in painting is drawing, the element which connects painting to discourse, and gives it a didactic role and an attendant moral message. The Academy thus became the bastion of drawing, which was defined as an abstract representation whose origins reside solely in thought, the mark of a purely intellectual activity that proves, to those who would condemn painting, that painting always follows a 'design' or project. The word for this activity at this time was either 'desseigner' or 'dessiner', the two terms being distinct neither in spelling nor in meaning.[24]

When, in the 1660s, the advocates of colour began to attack the primacy of drawing in painting, they were accused of threatening the nobility of painting, and of spreading erroneous and false principles. To attack the privileged place of drawing was to attack the Academy itself, which responded with all of the traditional philosophical objections to colour, which had long been associated with the senses and the fleeting, changeable, and thus deceptive, material world. In his response of 7 January 1672 to the colourist discourse of Gabriel Blanchard, J.-B. de Champaigne argued that the relation of drawing to colour is as the relation of form to matter, and as the relation of truth to accident. The end of painting, imitation, is superior to matter, which is used only as a means. To privilege painting's specific difference, colour, over its genre, imitation, would be to subordinate form or final cause to matter, against all the rules. Two days later, on 9 January, Le Brun insisted upon the accidental nature of colour, which is produced by light and changes with it.

But, in a publication career spanning the last quarter of the century and the beginning of the next,[25] and in a professional career which saw not only his eventual admission to the Academy, but also his development into its official theorist,[26] de Piles responded to the partisans of drawing point by point. To the old argument that colour is a mere seducer, what Blanchard had called 'la belle enchanteresse', the colourists replied that, thanks to colour, painting is a universal language and is able both to please scholars and to charm the ignorant. To the argument that colour cannot be taught by rules as can drawing, the colourists responded with the argument of genius. To the charge that the colourist is a mere dyer, dealing in base materiality which must be worked by the hand, the colourists responded with the quintessentially modernist argument that it is in fact drawing which is the work of the hand, and that drawing is but a potentiality which must be completed by colour, which comes second, and perfects it.

What is unprecedented in the criticism of de Piles, and what marks his production as a true shift in the history of the gaze, is his insistence upon the valorization of painting as such, and his rejection of the dichotomy substance–ornament, which had forever characterized colour as the latter. Whereas the Academy would ground painting's nobility in what it shares with architecture, sculpture and history, its 'dessein', which produced its moral value, de Piles claimed in the 1677 *Conversations* that 'la peinture est donc faite non pas precisément pour instruire comme vous l'asurez: mais pour representer les objets, & si un Peintre en representant vous instruit, il ne le fait pas comme Peintre, mais comme Historien'.[27] The valorization of colour, further, marks a philosophically unprecedented admission of the aesthetic value of seduction by the material world: 'L'oeil ne doit pas tant aller chercher le Tableau, comme le Tableau doit attirer l'oeil & le forcer, pour ainsi dire, à le regarder' (80). The advocates of drawing, then, claimed that painting's project is precisely not painterly, and has nothing to do with what makes a painting a painting and not a drawing. In exactly the same way, Aristotle's *Poetics* advocated poetry by claiming that its project does not necessarily depend upon poetry: 'All this shows that it is the plot, rather than the verse, which makes a poet' (1451^{b}).

And indeed, the name and authority of Aristotle were appropriated by the early Academy for the cause of legitimating painting as a function of drawing. The particular seventeenth-century reading of the *Poetics* dominated the Academy's first attempts to define the rules of painting, from about 1667, and unity of action remained an academic doctrine for a century and a half thereafter.[28] One would certainly expect to find Racinian poetics on the Aristotelian side of this battle. Racine's own conception of the tragedy, as in 'ma tragédie est faite', is clearly the Aristotelian one which would place him on the side of drawing, the institution, the discursive and the moral. Whereas for de Piles, the artist should begin not just with a proper conception of his subject but also with a specifically visual image of the work, for Racine as for the partisans of drawing, the mental and intellectual ordering of the subject matter was the true work of the artist.[29] Indeed, as if in affirmation of this position, the first words of *Phèdre* are 'le dessein', Hippolyte's 'Le dessein en est pris'.

Further, this 'dessein' which is the tragedy's first noun is to be regarded as being, in at least two fields, synonymous with the tragic action. Firstly, as I argued in Chapter 1, the Aristotelian poetics of the tragedy privilege its *corps*, which, in Furetière's definition, is composed of 'le dessein, la distribution'. But also, 'dessein' is the word in *Phèdre* which marks the distance between the ancient tragedy of Euripides and the tragedy of Racine with respect to the plot. Whereas in Euripides Hippolyte is accused by Phèdre of rape, in Racine he is accused only of having wanted to rape his step-mother: 'Mais il n'est ici accusé que d'en avoir eu le dessein.' Hippolyte, that is, has alleged designs upon Phèdre, and the difference between the ancient tragedy and the modern one is precisely in the design: the modern tragedy is designed to be a problem of designs.

This new 'dessein' of the tragedy leads to a new painting: since Phèdre accordingly does not hang herself at the tragedy's mid-point, as she does in Euripides, the project of the Racinian tragedy may indeed be said to be the action of her dying, which she herself urges the new accuser, Œnone, to paint for Hippolyte: 'Presse, pleure, gémis; peins-lui Phèdre mourante' (809).

Œnone's painting as a figure for rhetorical performance can in one sense be said to be a seventeenth-century commonplace. This was a moment when pictorial representation served as a paradigm for all systems of representation, and provided a general model for comprehending all forms of imitation.[30] But we should be attentive here to the fact that the figure of painting is being used not to comprehend a poetic performance in general, but rather a rhetorical one, one whose entire goal is to move Hippolyte to do as Phèdre wishes. This forthcoming rhetorical performance has as its most powerful techniques entreaty, tears and moaning, 'presse, pleure, gémis', that is, it includes eloquent bodily gestures which fall outside of the domain of language in a way that is both familiar and unsettling. While, as Hawcroft reminds us (4), the silently gesturing body is to be comprehended within the 'action' which is the fifth part of rhetoric, it is precisely not a rhetorical figure and is accordingly the object of much suspicion.[31] This suspicion plays itself out in *Phèdre* in the fact that Œnone never has the opportunity to deliver her speech to Hippolyte, being prevented from doing so by the tragedy's new mid-point, the return of Thésée. Rather, her rhetorical performance is of the accusation itself, an accusation which turns upon a silently gesturing body which is doubly interpretable, whose meaning is unfixed: the famous painting of Hippolyte's designs, 'J'ai vu lever le bras' (1019).

Phèdre, to this extent, can be seen to be engaged in the seventeenth-century equation between painting and rhetoric. And, while the equation between poetry and painting, the 'ut pictura poesis', was a commonplace of the Academy of Colbert and Le Brun, the equation between rhetoric and painting was central to the thought of de Piles.[32] 'Le Peintre est comme l'Orateur, & le Sculpteur comme le Grammerien,' he wrote in the 1677 *Conversations*. 'Le Peintre doit persuader les yeux comme un homme Eloquent doit toucher le coeur' (102). According to de Piles, it was colour which rendered the painting eloquent.

With respect to the visual component of Racinian tragedy, it has recently been observed that 'there was an alternative agenda subverting the decorous precepts of Aristotle'.[33] Indeed, for all of the strength of Racine's reliance upon the conception of tragedy taken from the *Poetics*, the question of the Racinian gaze does not produce a neat set of responses which would be consonant with the positions taken up by the partisans of drawing. Perhaps the most interesting possibility for the response of the Racinian gaze to the contemporary contest for vision among the painters is that the language of the tragedy, reduced to a 'reste', a 'rien', for Racine—'comptant le reste pour rien'—holds the theoretical and practical place in the tragedy that colour holds in painting. The language of the tragedy, 'composé pour le plaisir', represents the danger which colour represented for the Academy: that element which is the materiality, indeed the seductive materiality, of the representation, which takes it out of the world of ideas and into the world of the sensuous, whether sounding or visible.

The painter paints by means of colour just as the poet does by means of words. Indeed, colour is precisely called this 'reste' by one of the interlocutors whom de Piles sets up as a straw man in the *Conversations*: 'J'ay toûjours oüi dire à Rome que pourvue qu'un Peintre dessinast, le reste qui est peu de chose, alloit toûjours assez bien' (93). This 'reste' is the tragedy's pleasure, 'un style composé pour le plaisir', just as colour in painting is the locus of its sensory pleasure, as opposed to the philosophical truth contained in its drawing.[34] If this is the case, then the vocabulary of painting in *Phèdre* should show some trace of this structure.

In general, vocabulary of painting in *Phèdre* is associated with gestures of narration. Théramène's tales of Thésée's heroic exploits are called by Hippolyte, for example, 'Quand tu me dépeignais ce héros intrépide' (77). Occasionally, painting is a general metaphor for characterization, as in Hippolyte's 'Avec quelques couleurs qu'on ait peint ma fierté,/ Croit-on que dans ses flancs un monstre m'ait porté?' (519–20); or his 'Je ne veux point me peindre avec trop d'avantage' (1105). To be without colour, on the other hand, is to be speechless, as is Hippolyte before Thésée: 'Je vous vois sans épée, interdit, sans couleur' (715). But the true eye of drawing belongs to the one who has designs, to Phèdre herself, as, in her famous declaration scene, she sees the young Thésée as a painting of the gods, or of the present Hippolyte: 'Tel qu'on depeint nos dieux, ou tel que je vous voi' (640). This painting is first drawn, 'Il avait votre port, vos yeux, votre langage' (641); and then coloured in: 'Cette noble pudeur colorait son visage' (642).

In general, the only actual colours mentioned in *Phèdre* are red and black. Reddening always means blushing with shame, as in Hippolyte's 'Je commence à rougir de mon oisiveté' (4). Black and blackening weigh down the tragedy's second half: only one form of 'noir' appears in the first 827 lines, while, after the return of Thésée, blackness is used eight times.[35] Indeed, the action may be said to be characterized by and to end on this increasingly prominent blackness, with a colour rhyme: 'D'une action si noire/ Que ne peut avec elle expirer la mémoire!' (1645–6).

But there is one striking exception to all of these generalizations concerning the use of colour in *Phèdre*: the *récit de Théramène*. This long (1498–1592) recounting by Hippolyte's governor to Thésée of the circumstances of the prince's agony and death has historically been the most minutely analysed and energetically critiqued passage in all of Racinian tragedy, and I will turn to the history of its readings and further problems of its poetics in Chapter 4. But the *récit de Théramène* is also a central text for the question of the Racinian gaze. This is so because it is, in one important way, nothing at all but 'parler'. The quality of this 'parler', however, distinguishes itself in just the same way as does the accusation of Œnone. That is, the *récit de Théramène* carries the same rhetorical marker of 'j'ai vu': 'J'ai vu, seigneur, j'ai vu votre malheureux fils' (1547). It is thus the second example in *Phèdre* of that second kind of Racinian gaze, the hypotyposis, which 'sets the thing before the eyes', rather than the desiring gaze whose structure was exposed by Starobinski. And the link with the visual is reinforced by d'Aubignac's providing, as an example of speech as action, the narration of the death of Hippolytus in Seneca, which is 'l'Action d'un homme effrayé d'un Monstre qu'il a veû sortir de la Mer, et de la funeste avanture de ce Prince' (282).

The *récit de Théramène*, accordingly, is a rhetorical event which could be characterized as painting in the sense of 'Peins-lui Phèdre mourante'. This being the case, it is of the greatest interest to note that none of the generalities concerning the use of the vocabulary of painting and colour which is true for the rest of the tragedy holds true for the *récit*. 'Red' here is not a periphrasis for blushing: the horses redden the bit with bloody foam, and in the *récit* there appears for the only time in all of Racinian tragedy the word 'rouge': 'Elle approche; elle voit l'herbe rouge et fumante' (1577). Also, yellow is seen by Théramène, and by no one else on Racine's stage, in the yellowish scales of the monster: 'Tout son corps est couvert d'écailles jaunissantes' (1518). Suddenly in the *récit*, the tragedy is no longer colour blind. As for drawing, when Théramène does refer to the scene as an 'image', the image which causes him to cry is that of the prince tangled up in the lines: 'Dans les rênes lui-même il tombe embarrassé./ Excusez ma douleur: cette image cruelle/ Sera pour moi de pleurs une source éternelle' (1544–6). After the treachery of the reins, it is pure colour tinting the rocks which is the trace of Hippolyte: 'De son généreux sang la trace nous conduit;/ Les rochers en sont teints' (1556–7).

Given the restraint of the tragedy in general with respect to colouring, Théramène's *récit* bursts out of the text as though the tragedy had suddenly been colourized. The rhetorical event to which it is symmetrical is Œnone's accusation, which turned upon design, the 'dessein d'un amant furieux' (1015). It is as though colour has now come to repair the effects of a suspect rhetoric in black and white, and to affirm the colourists' claim that colour is the true condition of visibility of the object, and that its outline, its design, is but a variously interpretable potentiality.

The manner of Hippolyte's death has been a subject of great fascination for *Phèdre*'s readers from the moment of its première to the present. The monster's relation to Phèdre's monstrous passion has been enthusiastically explicated, Neptune's participation as the god of horses as well as of the sea has been emphasized, and the cruel irony of Hippolyte's very name has been pointed out. I would like to suggest, however, that it is the lines which killed him, the lines of the reins by means of which he was dragged to his death, and that this is perfectly consistent with the great question of the action of the modern tragedy, in contradistinction to the ancient one: who, exactly, has designs upon whom? It is designs, Phèdre's designs rhetorically imputed by Œnone to Hippolyte, which kill Hippolyte. What would then be exposed in the tragedy is a kind of verbal-visual logic. 'Dessein', having designs, and intentionality in general are painted in the colourized discourse of Théramène as what might be called the essence of drawing, the line. At the mention of this line, it is clear from the text that the discourse itself is stopped. That is, after the word 'embarrassé', 'entangled' or 'ensnared', out of which there stares its own etymology as a 'bar', there is a break during which Théramène weeps. Barrault suggested that this word be followed by a moment of absolute stillness on the stage while Théramène collects himself and finds the strength to continue.[36] What happens at that moment, then, is the height of a rhetorical performance by the silently speaking body. Théramène becomes but a mute visual image, a painting. At the mention of the lines, he becomes a demonstration of the equation between painting and rhetoric which is central to colourist theory, and the embodiment of the action which is completely constituted by speaking, but which is not speaking. This is rhetoric's moment; its aim is to move its spectators by seduction of the eye, a moment that colourist theory depended upon and elaborated. This is not a moment of intentionality or discourse, which is silenced. And it is certainly not a moment for line, which seems indeed to have killed the boy. Immediately following this moment, the quality of the hypotyposis is exposed to view by its marker, repeated: 'J'ai vu, seigneur, j'ai vu'.

In the second section of the *récit*, which begins with Théramène's

'J'ai vu', the dying Hippolyte is still formulated in terms of line and colour: he asks that Thésée act 'pour apaiser mon sang et mon ombre plaintive' (1565). But in the third section, which begins with the entrance of Aricie (1574), the quality of the gaze shifts. Théramène is still the voice of the hypotyposis, setting the scene before the eyes, the speaking painting who paints in colour, but what he is now painting is a gaze, Aricie's vision of the dead body of Hippolyte. This is a particular vision of a particular vision, and its question is: What does Aricie see? 'Elle voit' is three times repeated (1578, 1579, 1582). She sees 'Hippolyte étendu', and she sees the product of the hypotyposis, set before her eyes, 'il est devant ses yeux' (1583). But the object of her gaze, says Théramène, is 'sans forme et sans couleur' (1579). It is clear, then, that something else has happened to the Racinian gaze in this third section of the *récit de Théramène*. Whereas up to this point, the *récit* can be opened up to a reading which functions in terms of line and colour, its object has somehow managed to escape its terms at this point. Within the structure of what gaze, or whose gaze, can this object be seen?

The only possible answer to this question is that something so radical has happened to Hippolyte that he is simply gone. The rhetorical figure of hypotyposis undoes itself in this moment, and takes the thing away. This is the condition for Aricie's being 'too sure' that he is before her: 'Mais trop sûre à la fin qu'il est devant ses yeux' (1583). Before her eyes at this moment is what Thésée will call, in the tragedy's closing moments, 'ce qui reste' (1650). This 'reste' recalls the 'reste' which was the verse of the tragedy, its materiality, and the colour of painting, its materiality, but it has now somehow disappeared, having neither form nor colour, yet visible. In order to understand how this might be, we can take advantage of the fact that the two painters who were considered exemplary in the colour-drawing debate which was consuming the Academy at the time of *Phèdre*'s première, Poussin for the partisans of drawing, and Rubens for the colourists, each set the theme of the death of Hippolytus.

It seems to have been only Rubens and the French who set this theme. It was never taken up by the Italians, the Spanish or the Germans. From the French seventeenth century, in addition to Poussin's two drawings, there is only a copperplate engraving by Sébastien Le Clerc after Charles Le Brun, composed for the publication of *Phèdre*.[37] What can the treatment of this fragile moment by the two exemplars of painting's great battle against itself tell us about Racine's poetry and Théramène's rhetorical painting of a body seen 'sans forme et sans couleur'?

The Poussin drawing shows the scene of the chariot crash [Fig. 1]. The chariot is empty and leaning at a precarious angle at the base of a rocky outcrop. In front of the chariot are four horses in various postures of flight and alarm. A helmeted figure tries to steady the reins, while, behind him, a figure with the outstretched arms of panic plunges into the confusion. At the far right is the figure of an older man, holding the limp body of Hippolytus in outstretched arms, as though offering, or supplicating. Three elements are drawn more sketchily into the scene: some background trees, a classicizing temple and two figures reclining comfortably up upon the rock, watching over the scene.

With respect to composition, the Poussin drawing approaches Racine's tragedy more closely than does any work of Rubens, for it is in the same compositional tradition as is Le Clerc's engraving [Fig. 2]: here, the horses have collapsed in a heap, while one rears up and an attendant tries to steady it in the foreground; Hippolytus limply reclines with attendants in the middle ground, and in the background are the dead monster, a rocky outcropping on the shore and a classicizing temple. Given this compositional connection, it is of the greatest interest to note that Poussin has drawn another 'Death of Hippolytus' on the verso of the first [Fig. 3]. It is a rapid sketch of the same scene, but a different moment: with the upended chariot and rocky outcropping in the background, the body of Hippolytus lies stretched out on a little rise. A figure with arms extended stands above him, and below are two figures. The larger of the two inclines towards the body and holds out to him a stick around which is entwined a snake, while he reaches with his other hand for something which the other figure holds. This, as the sketch's commentators have noted, is Aesculapius. Both in *Metamorphoses* XV and in *Aeneid* VII, he brings Hippolytus back to life with the power of the herbs of his father Apollo, which, at the moment of this sketch, he is taking from the other figure, who may be Paean, the physician of the gods, according to the *Metamorphoses*, or perhaps Telesphorus, the boy genius of healing.[38]

These two figures provide a clue to the identity of the two spectators in the drawing, recto, for beside one is the outline of the same oval package of herbs as is carried by the attendant in the drawing, verso. It appears, then, that this drawing, while its subject may indeed be said to be the death of Hippolytus, is in fact just as much about his metamorphosis, his resurrection. This properly epic and mythological component played a prominent part in the construction of Hippolytus in the early modern period. Du Bellay's *Défense et Ilustration de la Langue française* uses the body of Hippolytus as a figure for fragments of the languages of classical antiquity: 'Et si vous espérez (comme fit Esculape des membres d'Hippolyte) que par ces fragments recueillis elles [les langues greque et latine] puissent être ressuscitées, vous vous abusez'.[39] In the illustrated Ovid tradition, one of the most famous of the Ovidian iconologies, the *Metamorphoseon Ovidianarum* of Crispin van de Passe,[40] chooses the scene of the resurrection, rather than the scene of the chariot crash, for illustration [Fig. 4]: over the body leans the bearded figure of Aesculapius, holding bunches of herbs, and beside him stands Diana, who, according to *Metamorphoses* XV, protected the resurrected Hippolytus from the anger of Dis by enclosing him in a mist, ageing him, giving him the new name of Virbius and transporting him to the valley of Aricia.

It is thus this epic and mythological tradition of Hippolyte's resurrection that Racine references in the character of Aricie. In the tragedy, Aricie is the index to, the reminder of, Hippolyte's afterlife. Racine's *Préface* is perfectly explicit on this point: 'Cette Aricie n'est point un personnage de mon invention. Virgile dit qu'Hippolyte l'épousa, et en eut un fils, après qu'Esculape l'eut ressuscité.' One component of the Arician gaze, then, is the Poussinesque vision of the scene: not the death of Hippolytus, but rather the resurrection. This is why she is never sure that he is before her eyes. She is either completely blind—'Elle voit Hippolyte, et le demande encore' (1582)—or too sure that she sees—'Mais trop sûre à la fin qu'il est devant ses yeux' (1583). This view of Hippolytus follows both a broadly christological model, and a teleological model which, in *Metamorphoses* XV, equates Hippolytus with Rome, also cured through the intervention of Aesculapius. Hippolyte, in this tradition, is gone, 'sans forme et sans couleur', because at issue is his metamorphosis.

Rubens' painting of the scene presents a complicated problem of quotation and transformation. From him, we have three versions of this scene as well as a motif study. In the Musée Bonnat in Bayonne there is a drawing of the chariot crash [Fig. 5], which is usually dated around 1610 or 1611, that is, in the years just following Rubens' return from Italy in 1608.[41] A drawing for the central figure of Hippolytus is in the Louvre.[42] And there are two paintings, one in oil on panel in the Courtauld Institute, London, which is variously called a sketch or a sketchy version of the scene,[43] and a finished oil painting on copper in the Fitzwilliam Museum, Cambridge [frontispiece].[44]

Further, as was characteristic of his lifelong practice of copying, recombining and transforming pictorial elements gathered from every stage of his visual experience, which is not unrelated to his status as one of the great collectors of the age,[45] Rubens in the *Hippolytus* quotes and reappropriates a number of paintings and drawings which he had encountered in his youth and during his stay in Italy. There are some highly paraphrased memories here of the Farnese Gallery in Rome: the two fleeing figures distantly recall the terrified Acis and Galatea, trying to escape the rock-hurling giant cyclops in what has been called the 'Polyphemus furioso';[46] and the Triton blowing a conch trumpet on the right may recall the 'Venus and Triton' from the same series. The horses derive loosely from Leonardo's cartoon for the Battle of Anghiari, of which Rubens left two copies, a drawing in the Louvre and a painting in Vienna.[47] The great bull charging out of the sea is the painting's most prominent non-Italian quotation: it quotes a drawing by Rubens after a woodcut by Jost Ammon in a 1580 edition of the *Jewish Wars* of Flavius Josephus.[48] But certainly the most striking quotation is that of the figure of Hippolytus, which, as was long ago noticed by art historians, follows the Michelangelo drawing of Tityus in the Royal Collection, Windsor [Fig. 6].[49]

Apart from this kind of source-critical and genealogical commentary, Rubens' *Hippolytus* project has not been the object of a great deal of attention from scholars, as have the great compositions of the Medici Cycle, the Kermis in the Louvre and the Silenus figures.[50] Svetlana Alpers once took up the mythological paintings from the years shortly following Rubens' homecoming, but she explicitly excluded the *Hippolytus*.[51] Accordingly, my project here will include a formal and conceptual analysis, seeking to understand how the reading of this painting may relate to the *récit de Théramène*. If the discourse of Théramène is indeed produced from within a colourist rhetoric, and if Rubens, in contradistinction to the ways in which he himself formulated his own painterly project, is the keystone of the French seventeenth century's construction of colour as the primary condition of seeing, and if the subject, the death of Hippolytus, provides a positive basis for a double analysis, what, then, can this painting tell us about the Racinian gaze?

A great deal of weight must be placed on the figure of Hippolytus. A formal analysis of the painting shows it to be broadly composed as a great 'X', with the line of the shore forming one diagonal and the line of the mythological action forming the other. The body of Hippolytus receives special emphasis in this composition, for it, and especially the clenched fist, is the apex of a conical design of action and opposing forces: from the monster charging from the sea, to the furious and panicked horses trying to avoid a head-on collision, through the broken chariot and finally to the gleaming body of the prince. Further, this brilliantly lit body is the painting's most radical departure from the drawn sketch. In the sketch, the body of Hippolytus parallels the shore; it is entangled in the reins as the figure in the painting is not; and it is arranged with legs wide apart and arms limply overhead. The sketched body of Hippolytus is clearly being dragged to death in a way that the painted body is not. The repositioning of Hippolytus brings the monster into the conical design, and creates the formal 'X' of the painting, for, in the sketch, it is clear from actual lines drawn in the composition of horses, chariot and body that the formal design is to be conical, but the monster in the sketch parallels the shore and is outside of the lines.[52]

The inspiration for this heavily accented body, as has been noted, is the *Tityus* of Michelangelo, one of a group of drawings that Michelangelo made and gave as gifts to a young Roman, Tommaso de'Cavalieri. The quotation from the Michelangelo drawing would at first seem to convict Hippolytus in a way that neither the tragic nor the mythological tradition does. For Tityus was a giant who assaulted Latona, the mother of Apollo and Diana, and was then punished by having his liver perpetually torn out by a vulture. Thus the *Tityus* has little to do with death, but rather with eternal suffering, and this is echoed in the biographical significance which art historians have generally found in the theme, since Michelangelo's attachment to the Roman boy is expressed as well in his poetry. It is probable that the *Tityus* was one of two drawings which Michelangelo presented to Cavalieri in the winter of 1532, the other being a Rape of Ganymede which is now lost, but is known from numerous copies,[53] one of which Rubens owned and retouched.[54] Critics have generally seen in this pairing an allegory of sacred and profane love, an interpretation which is reinforced by the suggestion made to Michelangelo by

Sebastiano del Piombo that he convert his figure of Ganymede into an image of St John the Evangelist ascending into Heaven.[55] Mythology, biography and source criticism thus all conspire to convict Tityus, and to support a reading of his image as one of lust suffering deservedly.

However, both the drawing itself and Rubens' reading of it suggest that this may not be so. Just as Poussin's *Hippolytus* has a verso sketch which helps to explicate its recto, the Michelangelo drawing of Tityus has a sketch on the verso [Fig. 7]. This sketch is not a continuation of the narrative, but rather a tracing. Michelangelo has held the sheet up to the light and traced Tityus on the other side, but has transformed the mythological figure into a resurrected Christ.[56] Thrown into question, then, is the guilt or innocence to be read in this figure. And more exactly, the problem posed by the transformation of this figure would be: what is the nature and quality of torment? If the same posture serves for the suffering of Tityus, stretched out beneath the crucifix-form of Michelangelo's enormous vulture, and for the surpassing of the torture as Christ triumphant, are we not to read suffering as a noble, indeed transfiguring, activity? All that can be said with certainty is that the two figures are mirror images of each other. It is the right arm of Tityus which is bound; it is the left arm of the risen Christ which is held aloft.

And it is this latter image which Rubens has quoted, the left arm of Hippolytus with the clenched fist from which the action of the painting is unleashed, a reorientation necessitated by the re-composition of the painting to bring the body onto the axis of the horses and the monster. Further, Rubens' additional quotations of the Tityus figure support the notion that its agony was read by him as transfigurative, indeed creative. In this same reflection, with light falling from the left and with left fist bound to rock, the *Prometheus Bound* in the Philadelphia Museum of Art [Fig. 8], which dates as well from the years immediately following Rubens' return from Italy, has been shown to be 'a kind of hieroglyph for the condition of the creative artist'.[57] Prometheus was understood as the first artist, who animated lumps of clay with the spark of his genius, and the thematic connection with Tityus is clear: both are pecked in the liver, considered to be the seat of that melancholic bile with which artists were afflicted.[58] And the connection to the *Hippolytus* is clear as well, if more generalized: this painting is precisely not a death of Hippolytus. Rather, it is the agony of Hippolytus, his suffering and his forthcoming resurrection. It is, further, a thinking-through in paint of the question of causality.

What kills Hippolytus, according to this painting? The question of cause-and-effect, a temporal one, is thought through in paint, I would say, in terms of form and matter. If, in the *récit de Théramène,* it is the reins, line, which ensnare the prince, and the telling of which causes Théramène to represent himself as a mute painting, the colourists' eloquent body, this is not at all the case in the Rubens. Indeed, one major change from the sketch is the elimination, in the painting, of the prince's entanglement in the reins. In the painting, it is rather the horses which seem to be entangled. It is unclear how the horses are going to drag the prince to his death if he is holding the reins in his right hand. Rather, it is his own cloak which is winding around his leg, and upon which he seems to be tripping or slipping. Hippolytus, that is, is being tripped up by red. Indeed, the position of the figure's legs has been changed from the Tityus model, whose posture required none of the foreshortening to be seen in the Rubens. And this is just red, a cloak or drapery which has no shape or form of its own and must therefore be nothing but matter. Hippolytus, according to Rubens, is going to be killed by colour. The bullish monster is charging from the sea, and it sees red.[59] Mere matter, mere effect, the ornament which is clothing has thus, by the argument of this painting, been transformed into cause, form, substance. It is exactly this sort of power, I would say, that predisposed the work of Rubens to lend itself so pointedly to the partisans of colour in the great debate to come in France.

The painting differs from the sketch of the scene not only in its realignment of the Hippolytus figure, but also in that the painting adds, in the bottom left corner, some seashells and marine creatures, and the Triton, blowing on a conch shell. The response of art historians to these additions has been either to claim that they are not by Rubens at all, or, their paternity confirmed, to suggest that they may be explained as a requirement of a particular patron, who would have been a shell collector.[60] Shell collecting, which seems to have begun during the Renaissance with trade to the East and West Indies, was particularly fashionable in the Low Countries at this time.[61] A concern with the notion of metamorphosis, further, is evident in the pictorial programmes of several surviving curiosity cabinets, which may be painted with scenes from Ovid,[62] or, in one case, contain an automaton in which moving figures perform a story from the

Metamorphoses.[63] Rubens himself owned a small quantity of shells.[64]

I would like to suggest, however, that there is more to these shells than mere decorativity or the requirements of a commission. A purely formal analysis shows that the conical composition of the mythological action is mirrored in the conical arrangement of the marine creatures. As though to mark and emphasize the correspondence, the most prominent shell in the display is perfectly cone-shaped: the lines of the shell, on both micro- and macro-levels, are the compositional lines of the painting.

Of all of the elements in the painting, the marine creatures seem most clearly not to participate in the painting's affect. They are somehow painted with a different eye, and they do not participate, as do the sky, the water and the horses, in what will later, with Ruskin, be known as the pathetic fallacy. This second visual rhetoric within which the shells function can be called emblematic. They probably do not reference any particular emblem, although such connections are certainly possible. The water salamander making a beeline for the sword of Hippolytus may reference the series of emblems aimed at those, particularly soldiers, who turn stormy weather, confusion and hard times to their own profit.[65] The turtle's emblematic meanings range from its shell as a burden of sin, to its shell as that virtue against which fortune has no power, to the pertinent advice that one's own home is the best and that one should remain, like the turtle, within it.[66] However, the shell display should be read, not as a composition of fragments, but rather, like its mirrored mythological other, as a scenario of the shell. The shell is a broad metaphor for appearance, change and the transitory accident of an earthly life which can be only a short stop on the journey to salvation. And, on this point, there is a specific emblem which documents the reading. Camerarius IV, 56, 'Semel emigrabimus omnes', pictures a display of shells on a coastline, with crabs attempting to take up residence in the larger ones [Fig. 9]. 'Never do we inhabit secure dwellings here', says the inscription, 'but from here will we all go forth to the heavenly realm of the highest.' The naturalia of the hyper-real shell display, then, interacts with the artificialia of the art-historical mythological action. It interacts formally as the mirror of its conical composition, and it interacts thematically, echoing the impression that this painting is not about death, but rather about transfiguration. It is emblematic, firstly, in this interactivity, this reflection of the mythological moment in the natural objects which gloss it and which create a circulation of meaning between text and gloss, between, that is, two radically different visual rhetorics.

The painting, then, would seem to be complete and integral in its meaning, to be interpretable as this circularity of the notion of transfiguration or metamorphosis between the shell display and the chariot crash. Yet there is a second, and more profound, sense in which the painting may be called emblematic. As has been noted, the generation of meaning in the emblem, its 'âme', was considered by its theorists to be a function of interactivity between the 'corps' and the words of the emblem. The words, within this structure, have the status of interpreters, or translators, of a meaning which remains virtual. Picture and gloss work together to create the horizon at which they both vanish. In the present painting the shell display has this status of translator, a figural moment in paint which is only a display of shells, yet suggests something beyond itself, both essential to the painting, yet somehow pointing outside of the painting, opening itself up to the viewer. How, we might ask, can this structure be depicted, be pictorially signalled? What is 'vanishing' in paint?

On the edge of the painting there is a third shell-form. This is the second element which is not present in the sketch, the Triton blowing on a conch trumpet. This shell takes up and transfigures the meaning of the shells on the shore. It is the local, marine trope for the trumpet of fame, as it is in Alciatus 133, where Triton is blowing upon the conch shell and is surrounded by a serpent with tail in mouth.[67] The conch trumpet, still a swirling shell, nevertheless produces its opposite. It is not a 'mere' shell, transitory appearance, but fame, permanence, immortality. Its medium is not form and colour but breath. The shell display and the signalling Triton are the only two passages of the painting which have no textual base. All the other elements, including the fleeing attendants, are mentioned in either Ovid or Virgil. At this, the painting's most painted point, however, what the Triton signals is that Hippolytus becomes discourse, precisely not a painting but rather a text.

This, then, is the second sense in which we may understand the Racinian gaze of the hypotyposis. The figure of Théramène himself is the tragedy's structural analogue of the painting's Triton. For it is only in the tragic tradition that the messenger or governor plays a part. In the mythical and epic tradition, Hippolytus tells his own story. Théramène, in the tragedy, holds the trumpet of fame, tells the tale, and is the most textual of painters, as Triton is the most painterly of mythographers. When he claims that Hippolyte is 'sans forme et sans couleur', we may understand that at work here is not just the Poussinesque vision of the resurrection and metamorphosis of Hippolytus. The disappearance which has occurred is, more profoundly, this emblematic one. The hypotyposis which sets the thing before the eyes, which paints it in both simple and complex ways, causes the thing to vanish. It is a necessary and consistent vanishing, with respect to emblem theory, a vanishing which precisely creates meaning. Words are shells, in this structure, shells both empty of the body which is the Prince and the *pictura*, and, at the same time, filled up with the breath of meaning.

Notes to chapter 2

1. Jean Starobinski, 'Racine et la poétique du regard', in *L'Œil vivant* (Paris: Gallimard, 1961), 69–90.
2. On hypotyposis, see Quintillian, *Institutio oratoria*, trans. H. E. Butler (London: Heinemann, 1920–2), 6.2.22; on enargeia, Quintillian, 6.2.32.
3. David Maskell, *Racine. A Theatrical Reading* (Oxford: Clarendon Press, 1991), 108.
4. On the Lacanian gaze, see, most fundamentally, Jacques Lacan, *Le Séminaire, livre XI. Les Quatre Concepts fondamentaux de la psychanalyse* (Paris: Seuil, 1973), and, most recently, Renata Salecl and Slavoj Žižek (eds.), *Gaze and Voice as Love Objects* (Durham, N.C.: Duke University Press, 1996).
5. François Hédelin, abbé d'Aubignac, *La Pratique du théâtre* (Alger: Jules Carbonel, 1927), 282.
6. Michael Hawcroft, *Word as Action. Racine, Rhetoric, and Theatrical Language* (Oxford: Clarendon Press, 1992).
7. See esp. ch. 2, 'Verbal Action and Rhetorical Theory', 12–60.
8. René Bray, *La Formation de la doctrine classique en France* (Paris: Hachette, 1927), 247.
9. The standard work on this subject is still Rensselaer W. Lee, *Ut Pictura Poesis: The Humanistic Theory of Painting* (New York: Norton, 1967).
10. See George Boas (trans.), *The Hieroglyphics of Horapollo* (Princeton: Princeton University Press, 1993).
11. On the structure of this interactivity, see Linda Freeman Bauer, 'Seventeenth-Century Naturalism and the Emblematic Interpretation of Paintings', *Emblematica* 3 (1988), 209–28; and 'Further Reflections on an Emblematic Interpretation of Caravaggio's Early Works', *Emblematica* 7 (1993), 217–37.
12. For all of the nuances of this development, see Daniel Russell, *Emblematic Structures in Renaissance French Culture* (Toronto: University of Toronto Press, 1995).
13. On the emblematic as a way of reading, see Daniel Russell, *The Emblem and Device in France* (Lexington: French Forum, 1985), 22; Peter Daly, *Literature in the*

Light of the Emblem (Toronto: University of Toronto Press, 1979), p. ix and *passim*. Specialized studies of particular works and genres include Françoise Bardon, *Le Portrait mythologique à la cour de France sous Henri IV et Louis XIII* (Paris: Picard, 1974); Walter Benjamin, *Ursprung des deutschen Trauerspiels* (Frankfurt-a.-M.: Suhrkamp, 1963); Georges Couton, *La Poétique de La Fontaine* (Paris: PUF, 1957); Kurt Weinberg, 'The Lady and the Unicorn, or M. de Nemours à Coulommiers: Enigma, Device, Blazon and Emblem in *La Princesse de Clèves*,' *Euphorion* 71 (1977), 306–35; Amy Wygant, 'Corneille, Rubens, and the Heroic Emblem', *Emblematica* 9 (1995), 111–32..

14. Russell, *The Emblem and Device in France*, 20 and *passim*.
15. John Landwehr, *French, Italian, Spanish, and Portuguese Books of Devices and Emblems 1534–1827* (Utrecht: Haentjens Dekker & Gumbert, 1976), no. 635.
16. Claude-François Menestrier, *Art des Emblemes* (1662, New York and London: Garland, 1979), 50.
17. Letter to Mme Marie Racine of 16 Jan. 1697. Racine prefers to replace the rat with a boar's head, and thus to destroy the homophony of the 'rat' accompanied by a 'cygne'. *Œuvres complètes* (Paris: Seuil, 1962), 537.
18. Margaret McGowan, 'Racine, Menestrier, and Sublime Effects', *Theatre Research International* 1/2 (1975), 1–13.
19. Nicolas Boileau-Despréaux, 'Discours sur le stile des Inscriptions', *Dialogues, Réflexions critiques, Œuvres diverses*, ed. Charles-H. Boudhors (Paris: Belles Lettres, 1960), 194.
20. On de Piles, see Bernard Teyssèdre, *Roger de Piles et les débats sur le coloris au siècle de Louis XIV* (Paris: Bibliothèque des arts, 1957); Thomas Puttfarken, *Roger de Piles' Theory of Art* (New Haven and London: Yale University Press, 1985); Jacqueline Lichtenstein, *The Eloquence of Color: Rhetoric and Painting in the French Classical Age* (Berkeley: University of California Press, 1993); Svetlana Alpers, *The Making of Rubens* (New Haven and London: Yale University Press, 1995), esp. ch. 2, 'Making a Taste for Rubens'.
21. Teyssèdre, 'L'établissement de l'Académie royale de peinture et sculpture', in *Roger de Piles*, 15–26.
22. Teyssèdre, 'Les Prémisses, l'enjeu', in *Roger de Piles*, 154–65.
23. Teyssèdre, *Roger de Piles*, 122 n. 2.
24. See Furetière, *Dictionnaire universel*, s.v. 'Dessiner'.
25. De Piles's publications, in chronological order, following the 1668 translation of Du Fresnoy: *Dialogue sur le coloris*, 1673; *Conversations sur la connaisance de la peinture*, 1677; *Dissertations sur les ouvrages des plus fameux peintres*, 1681; *Abrégé de la vie des peintres*, 1699; *Cours de peinture par principes*, 1708.
26. Puttfarken, *Roger de Piles' Theory of Art*, pp. ix-xii.
27. Roger de Piles, *Conversations sur la connoissance de la peinture, et sur le jugement qu'on doit faire des tableaux* (Paris: Nicolas Langlois, 1677), 106–7.
28. Puttfarken, *Roger de Piles' Theory of Art*, 1–37.
29. Puttfarken, *Roger de Piles' Theory of Art*, 45.
30. Lichtenstein, *Eloquence*, esp. ch. 5, 'The Pictorial Paradigm: The World as Painting'.
31. On the status of rhetoric in the 17th cent., the essential reference is Marc Fumaroli, *L'Age de l'éloquence. Rhétorique et 'res literaria' de la Renaissance au seuil de l'époque classique* (1980) (Paris: Albin Michel, 1994).

32. Lichtenstein, *Eloquence*, esp. ch. 8, 'From a Poetics of the Image to a Rhetoric of Painting'.
33. Maskell, *Racine*, 246.
34. Lichtenstein, *Eloquence*, esp. ch. 1, 'Eloquence and its Makeup'.
35. Bryant C. Freeman and Alan Batson, *Concordance du théâtre et des poésies de Jean Racine* (Ithaca: Cornell University Press, 1968), ii. 817–18.
36. Jean-Louis Barrault, *Mise en scène de Phèdre* (Paris: Seuil, 1946), 183.
37. A. Pigler, *Barokthemen. Eine Auswahl von Verzeichnissen zur Ikonographie des 17. und 18. Jahrhunderts* (Budapest: Verlag der ungarischen Akademie der Wissenschaften, 1956), ii. 124.
38. *Encyclopaedia Britannica*, 11th edn., s.v. 'Aesculapius'.
39. Joachim Du Bellay, *Les Regrets [...] suivi de La Défense et Illustration de la Langue française*, ed. S. de Sacy (Paris: Gallimard, 1967), 227.
40. Crispin van de Passe, *Metamorphoseon Ovidianarum* (Cologne, 1602) (New York and London: Garland, 1979).
41. Gustav Glück and Franz Martin Haberditzl, *Die Handzeichnungen von Peter Paul Rubens* (Berlin: Julius Bard, 1928), no. 65; on Rubens's Italian experience, see Michael Jaffé, *Rubens and Italy* (Oxford: Phaidon, 1977).
42. Glück and Haberditzl, *Handzeichnungen*, no.66.
43. Julius Held, *The Oil Sketches of Peter Paul Rubens* (Princeton: Princeton University Press, 1980), no. 245; Antoine, Graf von Seilern, *Catalogue of Paintings and Drawings at 56 Princes Gate, London* (London: Shenval Press, 1955–71), no. 19; Michael Jaffé, *Rubens. Catalogo completo* (Milan: Rizzoli, 1989), no. 143.
44. Jaffé, *Catalogo*, no. 144; C[raig] H[artley], *Treasures from the Fitzwilliam* (Cambridge: Cambridge University Press, 1989), no. 94.
45. See Jeffrey M. Muller, *Rubens: The Artist as Collector* (Princeton: Princeton University Press, 1989).
46. Charles Dempsey, *Annibale Carracci. The Farnese Gallery, Rome* (New York: George Braziller, 1995), 64.
47. C[raig] H[artley], *Treasures from the Fitzwilliam*, 91.
48. C[raig] H[artley], *Treasures from the Fitzwilliam*, 91.
49. The debt was apparently first noticed by Oldenbourg in an essay published in 1918. See Seilern, *Catalogue*, 32. On the drawing, see Michael Hirst, *Michelangelo Draftsman. National Gallery, 9 October-11 December 1988* (Milan: Olivetti, 1988), no. 43.
50. On the Medici Cycle, for all the necessary bibliography, see, most recently, Ronald Forsyth Millen and Robert Erich Wolf, *Heroic Deeds and Mystic Figures: A New Reading of Rubens' Life of Maria de' Medici* (Princeton: Princeton University Press, 1989); on the Kermis and the Silenis figures, see Alpers, *The Making of Rubens*, cited above.
51. Svetlana Alpers, 'Manner and Meaning in some Rubens Mythologies', *Journal of the Warburg and Courtauld Institutes*, 30 (1967), 272–95.
52. Seilern, *Catalogue*, 32, reports that there exists in The Hague a poor photograph of a large painting, now presumably lost, which is the version of the subject to which this sketch corresponds. For my purposes, such a painting would correspond to the Cambridge *Hippolytus* in the same way as does the sketch. The Musée Bonnat sketch and the Cambridge *Hippolytus* clearly share multiple and

major pictorial elements: the shoreline diagonal, the horses, the monster, the figures of fleeing attendants.

53. Hirst, 103.
54. Jaffé, *Rubens and Italy*, plate 30.
55. Hirst, *Michelangelo*, 106.
56. Hirst, *Michelangelo*, 103.
57. Charles Dempsey, 'Euanthes redivivus: Rubens's *Prometheus Bound*', *Journal of the Warburg and Courtauld Institutes* 30 (1967), 420–5.
58. Raymond Klibansky, Erwin Panofsky and Fritz Saxl, *Saturn and Melancholy* (London: Nelson, 1964), 58 and *passim*.
59. Here we may recall Le Brun's call to the study of drawing, 'afin de ne nous pas laisser submerger dans l'Ocean de la Couleur'. Discourse of 9 Jan. 1672, quoted in Teyssèdre, 179.
60. C[raig] H[artley], *Treasures from the Fitzwilliam*, 91.
61. Th. H. Lunsingh Scheurleer, 'Early Dutch Cabinets of Curiosities', in *Origins of Museums. The Cabinet of Curiosities in Sixteenth- and Seventeenth-Century Europe*, ed. Oliver Impey and Arthur MacGregor (Oxford: Clarendon Press, 1985), 115–20; Henry E. Coomans, 'Conchology Before Linnaeus', in *Origins of Museums*, 188–92.
62. Annalise Scarpa Sonino, *Cabinet d'amateur. Le Grandi Collezioni d'arte nei dipinti dal XVII al XIX secolo* (Milan: Berenice, 1992), 11.
63. Hans-Olof Boström, 'Philipp Hainhofer and Gustavus Adolphus's *Kunstschrank* in Uppsala', in *Origins of Museums*, ed. Impey and MacGregor, 98.
64. Muller, *Rubens*, 23.
65. Arthur Henkel and Albrecht Schöne (eds.), *Emblemata. Handbuch der Sinnbildkunst des XVI. und XVII. Jahrhunderts* (Stuttgart: J. B. Metzler, 1967), 736–8.
66. Henkel and Schöne, *Emblemata*, 607–12.
67. Andreas Alciatus, *The Latin Emblems*, ed. Peter Daly, 2 vols. (Toronto: University of Toronto Press, 1985), i. 133.

Figure 1. Nicolas Poussin
Death of Hippolytus, recto. New York: Pierpont Morgan Library

Figure 2. Sébastien Le Clerc
Frontispiece engraving after Charles Le Brun
from Jean Racine, *Phèdre & Hippolyte* (Paris: Barbin, 1677)

Figure 3. Nicolas Poussin
Death of Hippolytus, verso. New York: Pierpont Morgan Library

Figure 4. Crispin van de Passe
'Death of Hippolytus'. *Metamorphoseon Ovidianarum*, Cologne, 1602

Figure 5. Sir Peter Paul Rubens
Death of Hippolytus. Bayonne: Musée Bonnat

Figure 6. Michelangelo
Tityus. The Royal Collection

Figure 7. Michelangelo
Risen Christ. The Royal Collection

Figure 8. Sir Peter Paul Rubens
Prometheus Bound. Philadelphia Museum of Art

LVI. 57

SEMEL EMI-
GRABIMVS OMNES.

Hic nusquam certis habitamus sedibus, ast hinc
Ibimus ad superi cælica regna Dei.

P ATHE-

Figure 9. Joachim Camerarius
'Semel emigrabimus omnes', *Symbolorum et emblematum ex acquatilibus et reptilibus* (Nürnberg, 1604), IV, no. LVI

CHAPTER 3

Garden
Memory in the Labyrinth

In Chapter One, I observed that the figure of Flore in the Prologue to Lully's *Atys* functions as an index to the difference between the received text of Ovid and the project of the early modern *tragédie*. Flore represents the tragedy's language; she is the contemporary figure of the possibility that the exploits of heroes be told. As a second instance of this kind of indexing function, I noted in Chapter Two that Œnone's 'J'ai vu lever le bras', the suspect rhetorical imputation of designs to Hippolyte, concentrates the problem of design which, on the level of the plot, separates the tragedy of Racine from that of Euripides and Seneca: 'Mais il n'est ici accusé que d'en avoir eu le dessein'.

A third example of this kind of fragile but analysable structure situates itself in the scene of Phèdre's declaration of her love to Hippolyte in Act II, scene 5. This is the play's second staging of a breach in Phèdre's self-imposed silence. The audience to the first had been the nurse, Œnone; the audience for the third and final emission of the terrible truth will be Thésée. Roland Barthes once argued that *Phèdre* is a tragedy of the word, 'Dire ou ne pas dire? Telle est la question'—the Hamletization of *Phèdre*, we shall see, was not without precedent—and, further, that it is a tragedy precisely of these words in this scene: the stakes of the tragedy depend less on Phèdre's love than on her avowal of it. Barthes is accordingly sensitive to the status of II. 5, as a play-within-a-play, to Phèdre-thaumaturge and Phèdre-dramaturge: 'Phèdre se lie magiquement à Hippolyte par un jeu, elle *représente* son amour, son aveu est dramatique' (original emphasis).[1] This scene has prompted confessional statements from characters as diverse as Marcel Proust and Leo Spitzer. In *Albertine disparue*, Proust's narrator calls Phèdre's declaration 'une sorte de prophétie des épisodes amoureux de ma propre existence'; and, when confronted with Phèdre's vision of Hippolyte as a younger Thésée, Spitzer, in a parenthetical excursus on adultery, remarked that marital infidelity is but one form of marital fidelity, 'so true is it that love is "typologically monogamic"'.[2]

The scene's participation in the thematics of the monster—Thésée's monster-killing, Hippolyte's aspiration to monster-killing, Phèdre's becoming-monster—has escaped almost no one, but it is with respect to the site of Phèdre's imagined erotic enterprise, the fabled labyrinth of Crete, that the elaborate thematic readings of the scene find a favourite and congenial subject. This is especially true in the case of psycho-critical approaches. Charles Mauron remarked that the labyrinth is 'un symbole très archaïque des entrailles maternelles',[3] and went on to compare Hippolyte's task to those of Perseus or St George. For Francesco Orlando, the relation Labyrinth/Minotaur was one of the seven symbolic negations in which 'the themes of the tragedy [...] are all abstractly summarized'.[4] Even Roland Barthes allowed his reading to become thematic with respect to the labyrinth: Thésée is 'un héros proprement chtonien', 'héros labyrinthique', an example of *Phèdre*'s 'thématique très ample du caché' (113–14).

But the restriction of the labyrinth to the status of a theme cannot take account of its specificity as a site. In 1677, the date of *Phèdre*'s premiere, the labyrinth, in addition to being a fabulous ancient site, was a locatable place in the garden of Versailles. One of the great landscape gardener André Le Nôtre's earliest *bosquets* in the Petit Parc, the Labyrinthe[5] had probably been laid out in the mid-1660s, and, starting in 1672, it had been embellished with thirty-nine fountains illustrating fables, mostly taken from Aesop and Phaedrus. My argument here will depend upon a juxtapositioning of the labyrinth produced at the Hôtel de Bourgogne, and the contemporary imagination of the labyrinth as it was materialized in the garden. At both sites, garden and tragedy, the idea of the labyrinth became unhinged from the story of Theseus and the Minotaur, and was redeployed as the location of a radically different situation of memory and action.

Scholars have long understood the importance of this unhinging, in general. The uprooting of the stories of Latin antiquity, and their transformation into the loose canon of abstraction, was once formulated by Jean-Marie Apostolidès as a procedural mode of 'La Mythistoire'.[6] But what is the mechanism, we might ask, of this redeployment? To what point, exactly, does this redeployment relate? The labyrinth as a tragic and horticultural site is an index into an ongoing early modern transformation of memory, as it emerged from the ancient and medieval storehouses of places and images, and from Renaissance occult practices.[7] If Flore gives us the tragedy's theoretical specificity, and the complex of designs gives us its practice, then the tragedy gives itself to be remembered from within a particular and properly early modern mnemotechnical structure.

This cannot be a general inquiry into the problem of memory before Freud, however urgent and necessary that task might be. But the labyrinths in *Phèdre* and in the garden of Versailles can be read to see how, at a particular moment in the long trajectory from the artificial memory of Latin antiquity to the declaration of Pierre Nora that 'on ne parle tant de mémoire que parce qu'il n'y en a plus',[8] the heroic story of memory, that of Theseus and the Minotaur, was partly forgotten, partly recalled, and the project of memory itself re-configured. Perhaps it is the case that the normal condition of loss is to be generative. Blanchot indeed reminds us with respect to the great myth of humanist loss and despair that 'Ecrire commence avec le regard d'Orphée'.[9] What, then, begins with Phèdre's loss, if loss it is? Upon what is this loss founded? 'Et sur quoi jugez-vous que j'en perds la mémoire, Prince?'[10]

I. Rewriting the Labyrinth

Of the two ancient sources of the tragedy, it is only in Seneca that Phaedra declares herself to Hippolytus. In Euripides' *Hippolytus*, there is one declaration only: Phaedra tells the nurse of her incestuous love, and this scene is the font of the famous *lieu commun* of *Phèdre*-writing, 'You have spoken it [the name of Hippolytus], not I' (351).[11] Offstage, the nurse then betrays Phaedra's love to Hippolytus, and Phaedra, whom we see onstage overhearing his curses, dismisses the nurse, swears the chorus to silence, and hangs herself, leaving a tablet tied to her wrist accusing Hippolytus of rape. This is the midpoint of the action.[12]

In Phaedra's great central declaration scene as first written by Seneca,[13] Phaedra rushes onstage, faints, and Hippolytus gathers her up. Her passion is too great to be spoken; Hippolytus calls her 'mother' (608).[14] At this prompting, she corrects the apostrophe, firstly to 'Call me your sister, or call me your maid (*famulam*)' (611), then to 'your suppliant or slave' (622), and there is a final reference to her 'widowhood' (624). She declares that she will perform various deeds on his behalf, involving travel—'to go through drifts of snow' (613), 'to go through fire' (615)—and offers him political power. Hippolytus responds in a first refusal to understand her heart: 'I will myself/ take up my father's place, fulfil his role' (633), and, to her declaration of love, in a second refusal to understand: 'This love you rage and burn with, I take it,/ is proper for a wife, is for Theseus?' (645). To his rhetorical question, Phaedra then responds with the mighty theme of Hippolytus as the new Theseus, a hermaphrodite god who reappears rejuvenated in his son: 'I love Theseus' face—the way it looked/ in years gone by, when he was still a boy, [...] He looked like your Phoebe, or my Phoebus, or rather like yourself' (646–7; 654–5). There follows from this a past, contrary-to-fact condition: 'Had you sailed with your father into Crete/ my sister would have spun her thread for you/ in preference' (661–2). Throughout, Phaedra remains a follower, and declares herself utterly powerless to establish any destination which has not been pre-determined by the presence of Hippolytus: 'But I have no/ control over myself; I'll follow you/ even through fire and across raging sea,/ boulder, and torrent-ravished river-stream./ Where you step, there I will madly rush' (699–702). The hunter thus hunted, it is in response to this positioning of himself forever in advance, his itinerary forever reproduced, that Hippolytus draws his sword and threatens to sacrifice his queen to the goddess of the hunt.

Seneca's scene proved indelible for sixteenth- and seventeenth-century French tragedy writing. The play was rewritten for the stage six times in just over a century, between 1573 and 1677, and Seneca's powerful declaration scene was never cut. Robert Garnier (*Hippolyte*, 1573)[15] causes Hippolyte not just to double Thésée, but rather to exceed him:

> Sa taille belle et droite avec ce teint divin
> Resembloit, esgalée, à celle d'Apollin,
> A celle de Diane, et sur tout à la vostre,
> Qui en rare beauté surpassez l'un et l'autre. (254)

The play was seen twice on the stage of the Hôtel de Bourgogne prior to Racine's premiere: in 1634, Guérin de La Pinelière produced his *Hippolyte*,[16] and here, the declaration scene is delayed until the middle of Act III. His Phèdre plays the scene dressed in a hunting costume, and it is she, not Hippolyte, who is forever attempting to escape the stage: 'Mettez moy ce carquois que sans honte & sans crainte/ Je suive mon Chasseur à travers ces forests' (III. i), 'Ha laisse moy sortir que je suive Hippolyte' (III. iii). By 1647, and the *Hypolite ou le garçon insensible* of Gabriel Gilbert,[17] Phèdre was but Thésée's fiancée, not yet his wife. This understandably led to some changes in her declaration scene: here, Hypolite resembles his father not in body but rather in moral qualities, 'Je blasme avec raison cét inconstant espoux,/ Et i'aime ses vertus qui renaissent en vous' (56). Gilbert's Phèdre reasons that it is in fact by marrying Thésée, the husband of her sister, that she would be committing incest. She asks Hypolite to take her home to Crete to escape Thésée's 'amour brutal'.

Two settings of the play group themselves around Racine's 1677 production: the *Hippolyte* of Mathieu Bidar, which was produced in Lille in 1675,[18] and Pradon's 'double', *Phèdre et Hippolyte*, which premiered two days after Racine's *Phèdre*, on 3 January 1677, and broke all records for house receipts at the Hôtel de Guénégaud.[19] All three plays supply a lover for Hippolyte. In Bidar, the declaration scene, while preserving certain Senecan *topoi* such as Hippolyte as the second Theseus, consists mainly of Hippolyte's protestations that he is not free to love Phèdre, as his affections are engaged elsewhere. In Pradon's declaration scene Phèdre discovers, before declaring herself to Hippolyte, that she has a rival in Aricie. In her fury, she turns her declaration into a threat to kill not just herself, but also all of the remaining protagonists, and to Hamletize the play's ending, with only bodies littering the stage: 'Je puis tout perdre helas! dans ma fureur extrème' (1045).

But within this luxuriant, century-long growth of *Phèdres*, and specifically of Phèdre declaration scenes, what of the labyrinth? We have seen that, in Seneca's tragedy, the theme of Hippolytus as the replacement Theseus heading off into the labyrinth to kill the Minotaur, and returning with the help of Ariadne, is already a major presence. It is worth re-emphasizing as well that Seneca already has Phaedra hallucinating about travelling—into snow drifts, and through flames—at the behest of Hippolytus, as well as compulsively following him through other kinds of geophysical obstacles—the mad sea, mountain crags and swollen rivers. We have also seen that these Senecan themes persist in the French tragedies of the Phèdre-century. However, in the course of these rewritings, something curious begins to happen to Phaedra's Senecan itinerary: it gets longer, and, more significantly, it gets deeper. In addition to going through wave, mountain, snow and fire, Garnier has Phèdre going into deep caves; La Pinelière's Phèdre declares, 'Et ie verray pour vous le centre de la terre'. So, to the extent that the labyrinth in general participates in a thematics of the earth, we might say that, from 1573 to 1634, Phèdre had been flirting with the entrance to the labyrinth.

Of the three productions clustering in the years 1675–7, it is only in Racine's that the *topos* of the labyrinth is further developed in Phèdre's declaration scene. The Phèdre of Bidar and Pradon is a sedentary type; she has forgotten her favoured fantasm; she imagines no itinerary, but rather stands and holds her ground. Why, then, should Racine hark back to Phaedra's *Wanderlust*?

In Racine's version, Phèdre's declaration is set off from the tragedy which surrounds it. Tragic time now runs backwards; this is the flashback of a veteran of too many travels. Things proceed through the scene conventionally, for a while. There is the motif of interdiction on Phèdre's part, and Hippolyte's assumption that she is still in love with her husband. The weighty theme of Hippolytus as the second Theseus enters—with the difference that Racine has written over the double, hermaphrodite ressemblance of Theseus to both 'your Phoebe' and 'my Phoebus' as 'Tel qu'on dépeint nos Dieux' (640). As in Seneca, Phèdre revises the role of her sister with a past, contrary-to-fact condition: 'Ma soeur du fil fatal eût armé votre main' (652).

But Racine's re-writing then takes an unprecedented turn. With an emphatic marker, 'Mais non', Phèdre claims something which neither her personal myth nor any other writer of her tragedies has ever allowed to her: precedence. At first, it is precedence over Ariadne in the matter of the fatal thread:

> Mais non, dans ce dessein je l'aurais devancée:
> L'amour m'en eût d'abord inspiré la pensée.
> C'est moi, Prince, c'est moi dont l'utile secours
> Vous eût du Labyrinthe enseigné les détours. (653–6)

Into what position has Phèdre now pivoted herself? It seems that she has become her sister. In her 'L'amour m'en eût d'abord inspiré la pensée', Phèdre thus thickens and reduplicates herself. The entanglement of her tenses—now past conditional, now simple present, 'c'est moi'—however signals that this first fantasmatic representation is yet not sufficient. Some archaic remnant of Phèdre-the-traveller, Phèdre-the-huntress, reasserts itself in a second claiming of precedence:

> Un fil n'eût point assez rassuré votre amante.
> Compagne du péril qu'il vous fallait chercher,
> Moi-même devant vous j'aurais voulu marcher;
> Et Phèdre au Labyrinthe avec vous descendue
> Se serait avec vous retrouvée ou perdue. (658–62)

Phèdre enters the labyrinth. Having become Ariadne, and having found this not to be going far enough, she becomes Theseus. She turns the tragedy of her following into the tragedy of her leading: *devant vous*. Now in the position of the scout, even a fellow-hunter, *compagne*, the only remembrance of her ancient mad pursuit of Hippolytus comes with Racine's spectacular pun later in the scene: 'C'est peu de t'avoir fui, cruel, je t'ai chassé' (684).

Punning play is rarely noticed in Racine, perhaps because it is so rarely explicitly thematized in the tragedies. But, in these purely interpolated lines, the ultimate repositioning of Phèdre depends upon a similar kind of baroque effect. Having become Ariadne, and become Theseus, Phèdre's final move is to become herself, and the way that we know this is that she speaks of herself in the third person, alienates herself from herself: 'Et Phèdre au Labyrinthe ...'. But to call Phèdre 'alienated' is to borrow an anachronistic formulation of the state of madness. In more properly seventeenth-century terms, Phèdre uses the device of the mirror. She sees herself descended into the labyrinth as in a mirror, and in the resulting juxtaposition of *moi-même* and *Phèdre* becomes, finally, pure reflection, which is to say, pure theatre.

So all of the discursive weight formerly given to Phèdre's travels through fire, into caves, and so on, has been massively shifted onto a single heroic voyage, into the labyrinth. How does this newly constellated experience of the labyrinthine refigure the myth of Theseus and the Minotaur?

The traditional story of their confrontation would have been well known from Plutarch's *Lives*, and from Ovid's *Heroides* 10 and *Metamorphoses*, book 8. Theseus, son of King Aegeus of Athens, arrived in Crete as one of the Athenian youths paid as tribute every nine years to King Minos of Crete, a sacrifice exacted in vengeance for the death of his son, Androgeos. The sacrificial victims were sent off into the labyrinth, a 'many-folded house'[20] with blind passages and confusing, twisting ways, which had been built by the crafty trickster Daedalus. Hidden within was the shame of the kingdom, the monstrous, part-man, part-bull Minotaur, born following the disgusting love affair between Queen Pasiphae and a bull. No one except Daedalus himself had ever emerged from the mazy architectural masterpiece until Theseus, aided by the Princess Ariadne, reappeared in triumph. Out of love for him, she had given him a ball of thread which he used to retrace his steps, after killing the monster with his sword, and so to overcome the devastating complexity of the path. Theseus then fled with the princess, and returned home king of Athens, his father having thrown himself into the sea at the sight of the black sails of his son's vessel, which Theseus had 'forgotten' to change to white, as they had previously agreed would signal his safe return home. Ariadne was abandoned to die on the way.

This account of the Cretan labyrinth thus inserts one story of departure and return into a larger story of departure and return. It insists upon return; this is what the hero does. Cast out, sent beyond the pale of Athens, and given up as irretrievably lost, he returns as the defining and determining body of his city, its king. Cast into the labyrinth as Minotaur feed, he slays the semi-animal result of his lover's mother's lust, and returns not only unconsumed, but also transformed into a consumer—of princesses. He has become what he set out to slay, a divisible, bi-form creature, marked by what Racine's Hippolyte calls 'Cette indigne moitié d'une si belle histoire' (94).

In addition to this macro- and micro-tracing of the heroic departure and return, the story also promotes a particular notion of the way in which memory works. At both levels of the story, the heroic return depends upon forgetting. In Athens, Theseus would not have returned home as king had he not forgotten to hoist the white sails. In the labyrinth, the heroic nature of the return is also a function of forgetting. For Theseus, the combat with the Minotaur, his monster-killing and his monster-becoming, coincide with the onset of topological amnesia. Theseus annihilates not only the Minotaur but also his memory of the way out, and the thread, memorial prophylaxis, is pressed into service only when the deed is done. We might thus say that the combat has the status of pure event: it precisely *takes place*, and the place which it takes is the place of the map.[21]

Racine's rewriting of the mnemoscape of the labyrinth is radical. The hero Theseus is duplicated and reduplicated: explicitly as Hippolyte the rejuvenated Thésée, and implicitly as Phèdre the maze-treader, his 'compagne du péril'. The result of this double duplication is not, as might be expected, the concentration and elaboration of the heroic itinerary, but rather its permanent suspension. If the hero, in the traditional story, is collapsed upon his own return, defined, in one important way, as return itself, then the hero disappears from the labyrinth in *Phèdre*, put on permanent hold by the perfect equipoise of 'retrouvée, ou perdue' (662). The line which begins with a hiss and a stutter, 'Se serait avec vous ...', ends itself and Phèdre's labyrinth story with the question of loss or finding again which is the very question of the project of memory.

If the hero's return ceases to be the story's armature, then the mechanism by means of which that return is accomplished, the mechanism of forgetting and the whole mnemotechnical apparatus of the story, becomes estranged and available for reinterpretation. In Racine's version, the thread from the old story is reinterpreted in the space of a single Alexandrine: 'Un fil n'eût point assez rassuré votre amante' (658). Not exactly eliminated, the thread is rather declared inadequate. The old technology does not address the new difficulty, and it is, moreover, difficult to say what the new difficulty is. Both interlocutors accurately sense that something has been forgotten or lost here, but that something can no longer be confidently named 'the path'. This problem of the newly equivocal and suddenly unfindable status of what has been lost and forgotten forms the substance of the questions which Phèdre and Hippolyte ask each other following her new labyrinth story. Is this a place of forgetting, or a place of remembering all too well?

> Madame, oubliez-vous
> Que Thésée est mon père et qu'il est votre époux?
>
> Et sur quoi jugez-vous que j'en perds la mémoire,
> Prince? Aurais-je perdu tout le soin de ma gloire? (663–6)

If the hero is not necessarily coming back, and if the thread is not adequate to substitute for lost memory, the content of which is now truly irretrievable, then the mnemodynamics of the story change. The new maze-treader is under-insured by the thread. In the new labyrinth, this insurance gap is filled by Phèdre's *récit* itself. It is explicitly for her language that she claims sufficiency: she calls her imagined erotic enterprise 'enough', 'assez': 'Je t'en ai dit assez pour te tirer d'erreur' (671).

What seems to be at work here is no longer forgetting but rather something like un-remembering. This un-remembering extends itself to all components of the labyrinthine constellation: not only are the hero's return and the thread radically reinterpreted, but so also is the monster, which is no longer the site of combat, but rather the site of compulsive seeking. Accordingly, the direction-reversing and memory-annihilating centre of the labyrinth disappears. We might say that in the new labyrinth, it is ultimately the labyrinth itself, as mnemoscape, which is un-remembered. Racine's rewriting of the story has reconfigured not only its event structure and character distribution, but also the map within which the story occurs. The labyrinth of Phèdre's declaration scene presents not just a new mnemodynamics, but ultimately a radically refashioned site of memory and action, a new mnemonic topology of the labyrinthine.

II. Replanting the Labyrinth

We know that André Le Nôtre came to work at Versailles sometime shortly after the upheaval at Vaux in the late summer of 1661.[22] But the *bosquet* of the Labyrinthe emerges indistinctly with respect to its form and presence in the garden of Versailles. One scholar has gone so far as to suggest that the Labyrinthe was originally conceived for Vaux but executed only later at Versailles.[23] By some point around the middle of the 1660s it probably existed, and by the time that Madeleine de Scudéry wrote *La Promenade de Versailles*, perhaps around 1668 (since it was published in 1669), we know that the Labyrinthe was in place, since she explicitly mentions it.[24] The history of the place of the labyrinth in the pleasure garden, in general, is similarly enigmatic. Although the sign of the labyrinth is of great antiquity and has been the object of many a scholar's fascination, the origins of the courtly tradition of maze-treading in the aristocratic garden are quite unknown.[25]

The first representation of the park clearly to show the Labyrinthe in a form closely related to the *bosquet* later to be described by Perrault is a map in the Cabinet des Estampes [Fig. 10]. But the form taken by the paths on this map is nevertheless unique: there is an extra exit to the Northwest, on the side of the *bosquet* leading to the fountain of Bacchus, and the third meander is non-identical with its later form. The next representation of the Labyrinthe which has come down to us is a 1674 engraving of the gardens by Israel Sylvestre [Fig. 11]. It shows the paths of the Labyrinthe to be almost identical to those in Sébastian Le Clerc's engraved map which was to accompany Perrault's 1677 *Labyrinthe de Versailles* [Fig. 12]. And what had begun to be apparent from the earlier maps is confirmed by Sylvestre's map: in contradistinction to what the surviving traces show us of the organization of every previous garden labyrinth, this labyrinth at Versailles had no centre.

This raises several questions. Firstly, with respect to the overall plan of the garden of Versailles, we might wonder what the status of this un-centred place of convoluted asymmetry might be. What is it doing there, in this particular context, rather than outside it, or in some other? Secondly, what might the experiential topology of a centreless labyrinth be? If treading the maze had always in principle meant arriving sooner or later at its centre, reversing directions, and then exiting through its entrance, what might it mean to abandon circuitry in favour of linearity? Is there then a new mnemoscape, or has the labyrinth completely lost its memory?

In addition to the properly iconographic remains of the Labyrinthe, three other kinds of texts describe it in terms of their own. There are administrative records, the letters of Colbert to his shell and rock supplier in Marseilles, requesting shipments of these raw materials for the construction of the *bosquet*;[26] and the *Comptes des bâtiments du roi*, listing the payments to various artists and artisans for their work.

Also, there are guidebooks, which lead the visitor through the Labyrinthe and then subsequently remain as a souvenir of the trip. These range from the mannered and fanciful, such as Charles Perrault's 1675 'Le Labyrinthe de Versailles', which erects a complicated superstructure of gallantry over the map of the *bosquet*,[27] to the obsessively scopic, such as the 1677 *Labyrinte de Versailles*, which includes a map, two series of prose descriptions by Perrault, engravings by Le Clerc and descriptions cast into quatrains by Isaac de Benserade. The guidebook may be loquacious, even chatty, as are these latter two, or it may be dense, enigmatic and brief, as is the reference to the *bosquet* of the Labyrinthe in the *Manière de montrer les jardins de Versailles*, a record of the standard garden tour as it was set down by Louis XIV himself.[28] In a final category are the quatrains of Benserade, which belong both to the guidebook and to the *bosquet* itself.

By the time that Silvestre's engraved map appeared in 1674, the Labyrinthe had been embellished and recorded in various ways. The *Comptes des bâtiments du roi* show that, starting in 1672 and continuing through 1681, the *bosquet* had been an elaborate construction site. Most of the work seems to have taken place in 1673 and 1674, and it consisted of the installation of two statues at the entrance,

39 fountains, each one purporting to illustrate a fable of Aesop, benches and trellises, and signboards ('écriteaux', 139) at the entrance and on each of the 39 fountains, upon which Benserade's quatrains were inscribed in letters of gold. Some 45 workers are mentioned by name. They are the sculptors, rock-workers, metal-workers, locksmiths, tinsmiths, woodworkers, joiners, carpenters, plumbers, specialists in painting the sculpted birds and animals of the fountains, the 'voiturier par eau' who brought rocks from Fontainebleau to St Cloud, someone paid 'pour conroy'[29] and one La Perdrix who was paid 50 livres for a bird. It was a large and complex project, but it was only one of dozens of ambitious building projects ongoing in the garden at this time. There is a story that Le Nôtre was one day walking through the garden with the king, who gave the same cheerful answer to every proposal of his: 'Le Nôtre, I will allow you 10,000 francs for that.' After a series of such appropriations, however, Le Nôtre suddenly stopped and exclaimed, 'I will not say another word, or I shall be the ruin of your Majesty.'[30] Apocryphal or not, the little tale at least correctly posits the great landscape gardener as the prophet of the French monarchy's headlong rush to financial ruin, in which the *bosquet* of the Labyrinthe fully participates.

Nevertheless, it has been the sense of a variety of its observers, both its seventeenth-century contemporaries and its twentieth-century historians, that the Labyrinthe does distinguish itself from the rest of the garden. In the twentieth century, the great garden historian August Grisebach noticed its lack of a centre in these anxious terms: 'Statt des einen Mittelpunkts, der dem Gefangenen immerhin eine gewisse Direktive gab, trifft er jetzt auf verschiedene, scheinbare Zielpunkte hintereinander, so dass jede Orientierung unmöglich wird' (83).[31] This impossibility of orientation creates a lawless and orderless world which is different from the rest of the park: 'Das Gefühl, in eine enge, ordnungs- und gesetzlose Welt geraten zu sein, musste den, der aus den regulären, klaren Verhältnissen des Parks kam, ganz besonders berühren' (84).[32]

The maze-treaders of the seventeenth century do not seem to share Grisebach's anxious claustrophobia, but they do agree that the Labyrinthe is different. The 1677 *Labyrinte de Versailles* appeared in a polylingual edition (French, English, German, Dutch) from Nicolaus Visscher in Amsterdam in 1682, and the address to the English-language readers puts this difference in these terms (I extend the quotation to include the pun which writers about labyrinths in

English are apparently helpless to resist): 'Other representations are commonly estiemed because they please the eye, but this because it not onely delights the eare and eye, but together instructeth and edifies te hart and soul. This Labyrinth is seated in a wood so artificially and pleasant, as Dedalus him self would have stood amazed to behold it.' This is emphatically not Grisebach's narrow world lacking in law and order. Rather, it is a representation which distinguishes itself by the range of its sensory delights for the body, and its coincident ability to teach the whole man, heart and soul. Delight extends itself from the eye to include the ear, and the reference may be not only to the kind of white noise which would have been generated by the sound of so many fountains operating in such close proximity. But also, there may have been various naturalistic animal noises produced by the hydraulic machines. We know, for example, that at the last fountain before the exit, *Les cannes et le chien*, the small water dog which chased the ducks round the fountain's basin in a circle, actually barked.[33]

Charles Perrault's is clearly a seventeenth-century formulation of the labyrinthine difference in that his is also a Labyrinthe *in bono* and not, as is Grisebach's, *in malo*. By the time that his 'Le Labyrinthe de Versailles' appeared in 1675, Perrault had been secretary of the Petite académie since 1663, and premier commis des bâtiments royaux since 1665. He had been elected chancelier of the Académie française in 1672, and, in a highly unusual move for the Académie, re-elected the following year. In sum, he was a powerful courtier, highly favoured by Colbert. 'Le Labyrinthe' had been circulating in manuscript at court since 1673, probably in a non-explicit competition with the quatrains that Benserade must just at that time have been composing for inscription in the *bosquet*. Marc Soriano points to Perrault's fearless competitiveness as yet another sign of his confident position, while noting the fact that he lost this competition as an early warning sign of his forthcoming political demise.[34]

'Le Labyrinthe' is thus the product of a particular positioning in the institutional structure of the arts establishment. Profoundly the work of an insider, its determining conceit is one which it shares with an entire range of representations contemporary with it, most notably the paintings of Jean Cotelle the Younger: the gods inhabit the garden. In Perrault's garden, Amour one day meets Apollo, 'qui se promenait dans les beaux jardins de Versailles, qu'il aime maintenant plus qu'il n'a jamais aimé l'île Délos' (240). Amour, a skilful courtier, senses that the moment is right to ask that a favour be granted, and launches into an oration. 'Je vois que toutes les choses se font ici sous votre nom et si je ne me trompe, sous votre conduite', he begins (240). This is Amour making a rhetorical bow, placing the mythological setting of the Petit Parc under the sign of Apollo. The reference is most obviously to the garden's powerful central spine, marked by Tuby's Apollo rising from the waters of the Bassin d'Apollon to the west, and by the Grotte de Thétys, where nymphs bathed the tired god after his long day's work, to the east.[35] The moment then arrives for Amour to request the boon: 'Quoi qu'il en soit, reprit l'Amour, je vous laisse toute la gloire et consens que vous ordonniez de toutes choses, pourvu que vous me laissiez la disposition du Labyrinthe que j'aime avec passion, et qui me convient tout à fait. Car vous savez que je suis moi-même un labyrinthe, où l'on s'égare facilement' (240).

The most basic observation to be made about Perrault's formulation of the labyrinthine difference is that the Labyrinthe is non-Apollonian. Apollo may order all else in the garden, but the Labyrinthe belongs to Amour. What Grisebach calls 'the regular, clear relationships of the park' do not hold in the Labyrinthe, 'où l'on s'égare facilement'. Amour has a plan for his domain, corresponding to the rhetorical moment of *dispositio*, 'la disposition du Labyrinthe':

> Ma pensée serait d'y faire quantité de fontaines, et de les orner des plus ingénieuses fables d'Esope, sous lesquelles j'enfermerais des leçons et des maximes pour la conduite des amants; en sorte que comme ces divers ornements de fontaines serviront à faire retrouver l'issue du Labyrinthe à ceux qui s'y seront égarés, mes maximes contenues sous ces fables, serviront aussi aux amants pour se tirer d'une infinité d'embarras où ils se trouvent tous les jours. (240–1)

It seems safe to say that Perrault's text should be understood as broadly allegorical. In order to understand the situation of the Labyrinthe, it is necessary to sort out the various structures within which Perrault's allegory works. If the Labyrinthe is not Apollonian, what is it?

A first structure would be literary: in the gods Apollo and Amour there is a face-off between two different texts. The park is the place of Ovid, from whose *Metamorphoses* were taken the stories of the god Apollo, while the Labyrinthe is not the Ovidian labyrinth of Theseus and the Minotaur. Rather, it is the place of the fables of Aesop. A second structure would be the epistemological. The park is self-evident, a place of open meanings. But in the Labyrinthe the system of knowledge relies upon hidden meanings, maxims underneath fables. The Labyrinthe is didactic in a way that the rest of the park is not; it is a place where the moral may be learned. At the same time, however, it is confusing: the park is where Apollo is represented, but the Labyrinthe is where the erotic is self-identical, a narcissistic construction for the god of love himself: 'Car vous savez que je suis moi-même un labyrinthe'. Finally, there is the political structure of the allegory: the park is where the monarch is represented, but the Labyrinthe belongs to the courtier.

The moment of the visit to the Labyrinthe in Louis's *Manière de montrer les jardins de Versailles* is related to this latter allegorical structure. In one of its versions, the manuscript reads simply, 'On entrera dans le Labirinte, et après avoir descendu jusques aux canes et au chien, on remontera pour en sortir du costé de Bachus.'[36] Curiously, what never enters the Labyrinthe segment of the tour are the verbs of seeing and considering which dominate the rest of the text: 'on s'arrêtera pour considérer', 'on fera une pause pour voir', 'on fera voir', 'on fera considérer', 'on verra le costé' and so on. The most complicated movement of the garden walk, and the *bosquet* in which, it is safe to say, there is the most to see, elicits no seeing, and no command to others to see, from the King. On the contrary, the entire experience of the Labyrinthe is literally *après-coup*: one no sooner enters than it is all over, 'après avoir descendu'. One reason for this might be that, by the time that Louis first began to set down the *Manière* in 1689, the mood and tastes of the court had changed, and the Labyrinthe was not only out of fashion, but also something of an embarrassing reminder of the old days, and what was now perceived as their licentiousness.[37] But a more interesting explanation would accord with the implications of the political structure of Perrault's allegory. It is tempting to say that the Labyrinthe was the place in the garden where the King, as is accurately reflected in the *Manière* text, could not see. But more precisely, following Perrault's political alignment of the Labyrinthe, it seems to have been the one place in the garden where Louis *could not be seen*, and therefore, but only as a result of this state of affairs, was unable to see. The problem is that, in the Labyrinthe, there is no perspective. It may be theatrical, in a profound sense, but it is not stage-specific: it is not organized around a theoretical vanishing point. Other garden structures may remain unconsidered for various other reasons, but only the Labyrinthe is fundamentally unconsiderable, unassimilable to the structure of absolute monarchy, which, in the garden, quite literally requires perspective.

Given these multiple parameters of its difference, it seems clear that the Labyrinthe was marked off from the rest of the Petit Parc in the imagination of its contemporaries. It was the clausula of Versailles, a place both clearly inside the park, and yet, in many ways, outside of it: outside its mythological setting, and outside the most important assumptions about what it meant to be in and move through the garden. This imaginary placement found concrete expression in the employment of those locksmiths mentioned in the *Comptes des bâtiments*: although the rest of the park was not closed to the public until 1685, the Labyrinthe had from the beginning been fenced off, its entry barred by a locked gate, accessible only to those possessing a key.[38]

The second question, now: what does it mean to enter the Labyrinthe? One activity pursued in this *bosquet* built at the height of the power of the king's third great love, Mme de Montespan, was what a later generation would call 'indecency'. In 1739, in the course of a general repairing and repainting of the fountains, Louis XV had the hornbeam hedges destroyed, 'pour empêcher les indécences que leur épaisseur occasionnait'.[39] But these 'indecencies' were beside the point of the problem raised by the map of the Labyrinthe, that is, its lack of a centre. This centrelessness relates most closely to the problematic of memory and the question of the thread, to the mnemoscape presented to the maze-treader.

The entrance to the *bosquet* exposed the theory of the maze, and described the parameters of the experiential topology to come. Its extant iconographic fragments are a painting by Cotelle now in the Galerie du Grand Trianon [Fig. 13], and the engraving of Le Clerc in *Labyrinte de Versailles* [Fig. 14]. A painted lead sculpture stood on either side of the entry path, an Amour by Tuby to the left, and an Aesop by Le Gros to the right, following Le Clerc. Their positions are reversed in the Cotelle painting.

The two entry figures are indicators that the Labyrinthe has not lost its memory, but rather has been conceived from within a long history of fascination with its powers. In the discursive tradition of the Labyrinthe entrance, the hunchbacked figure is always identified as Aesop, but the winged figure opposite him did not always impress its reporters as Amour, or Cupid: at least one map of the Labyrinthe identifies the figure as 'la prudance sous la figure d'un Ange'.[40] This reference is to Cicero's categorization, in the *De inventione*, of memory as the third part, along with *intelligentia* and *providentia*, of one of the four cardinal virtues, prudence.[41] The Ciceronian text, the 'First Rhetoric' or 'Old Rhetoric' of the Middle Ages, was one of the two texts of Latin antiquity which drove the great medieval transformation of memory from a rhetorical problem to an ethical one.[42]

Through this medieval notion of an ethics of memory, the labyrinth gained the potential of losing its centre. This development in France, however, is traceable not just in the history of the formal garden, but also in the history of the festive royal entrance, and specifically in the entrance of the new queen Marie de Médicis into the city of Avignon in the year 1600, the title of which was 'Le Labyrinthe royal de l'Hercule gaulois triomphant'.[43] In this royal labyrinth, the Gallic Hercules is Henri IV, and the Queen proceeds through the city from arch to arch, each of which takes as its theme one of the labours of the new Hercules. The Queen in this case is not Theseus: there is no monster to be slain and no centre to this labyrinth. Rather, she proceeds through the cityscape in her triumphal chariot as the thread of Ariadne, her very body become the memorial link of the French monarchy: 'Cette Ariadne Françoise [...] doibt estre l'instrument, & le filet qui conduira ce grand Roy à cette immortalité d'une tres-heureuse, & feconde posterité' (55). But neither is Henri IV Theseus. Rather, the seven triumphal arches equate seven of the labours of his reign with the seven labours of Hercules, the ethical meaning of whom is the attainment of glory and immortality by toil and suffering.[44] 'Labyrinthe' in this case, then, is not just a generic name for a progression through the city. The issue here in the sense of its problematic is precisely not its issue in the sense of exit or outcome. In the labyrinth of the Avignon royal entry we can observe a complicated counterpoint between the sites and images of the artificial memory inherited from Latin antiquity—each of its seven arches would thus be a memory site—and the ethical memory of the Middle Ages, in which the process and progress through was indeed the issue.

The Labyrinthe of Versailles, then, in its very centrelessness, its unhinging of itself from the myth of Theseus and the Minotaur, represents a continuity with the ancient and medieval labyrinth of memory. It is a labyrinth of the ethical, each of its memory sites representing a task completed by the hero. We gain from the Avignon entry a good hint of the reflexive status of the ethical labyrinth: Memory itself, the mnemotechnical thread represented by the body of the Queen, issues forth triumphant.

And yet, as we have seen, the Versailles Labyrinthe, as all of its observers have noted, distinguishes itself. As a memory site, this distinction is thematized at its entry as the broken thread in Benserade's quatrain:

> L'Amour: Oui, je puis desormais fermer les yeux et rire;
> Avec ce peloton je saurai me conduire.
> Esope: Amour, ce foible fil pouroit bien t'egarer
> Au moindre choc il peut casser.

Tuby's Amour holds out a ball of thread to the maze-treader. It is this 'peloton' which Aesop declares to be not just inadequate but worse than useless. This is a thread which potentially leads astray, 'égarer'. In the old labyrinth, it was the annihilation of memory which was the problematic dysfunction, and it was this problem which the thread addressed. The new dysfunction is a technical problem posed by the former solution: the thread might break, and it might lead the maze-treader astray. One cannot have any confidence, at all, in mnemotechnics.

So, if the maze has no centre and thus no discrete monster; if there is no question of memory annihilation and reversal of direction; if the trusty old mnemonic device is now but a hindrance: then how is one to get through? The sources all agree that the new labyrinthine experience is a heuristic one. The Labyrinthe, as the Visscher guidebook put it, 'instructeth and edifies te hart and soul'. The new path is not, as was the old, impossibly complicated. Rather, it is quite possible, its detours are negotiable, but only according to the limits and rules of a knowledge structured in a particular way.

The statue of Aesop at the entrance held out to the maze-treader a roll of paper, a metonymy for the body of knowledge generally represented by fables. Perrault's 1675 quatrain for the statue emphasizes that teaching here will be achieved through the techniques of 'ruse' and 'adresse':

> Avec mes animaux pleins de ruse et d'adresse,
> Qui de vos moeurs font le vivant portrait
> Je voudrais bien enseigner la sagesse,
> Mais mon voisin ne veut pas qu'on en ait. (241)

It seems that the role of the new maze-treading hero, expressed here in the metre of epic poetry, is not to find the monster but rather to find himself: to find his own portrait in the animals of the fountains, and to learn 'sagesse', which is one possible translation of the Ciceronian 'prudentia'.[45] In 1675, Perrault situated the two entry figures agonistically. Aesop was the pure didact, but Amour, 'mon voisin', claimed, in the mixed metre of lyric poetry, to supersede the purely didactic by a combination of erotics, 'qu'on aime', and prudence, 'qu'on soit sage':

> Je veux qu'on aime, et qu'on soit sage,
> C'est être fou que n'aimer rien;
> Chaque animal le dit en son langage
> Il ne faut que l'écouter bien. (241)

The antagonism between the two figures thus establishes itself not over the content of the experience of the labyrinth, but rather over the mode of the perception of that content. Aesop is the figure of a primarily visual mode of teaching. In his quatrain, his animals are living portraits. The threat which he produces of the broken thread is in response to Amour's assertion that Amour can close his eyes: 'Je puis desormais fermer les yeux'. Amour, on the other hand, is the figure of hearing. His lyric metre asks to be sung; his animals speak, each in its own language; and the content of the labyrinthine experience is explicitly to be heard. In this, we encounter a formulation which will be confirmed by the 1682 Visscher guidebook: 'Other representations are commonly estiemed because they please the eye, but this because it [...] delights the eare and eye.' What this means is that a displacement has occurred. No longer is the question of the labyrinth whether or not the maze-treader will negotiate its intricacies. Rather, the question is now the properly ethical one of how that negotiation will occur. A disappearance of the labyrinthine as a site, as an inert context for action, is being effected by this displacement. Indeed, in two short years, by the time that *Labyrinte de Versailles* appears in 1677, the theory of the labyrinth declared by its entry figures has pluralized the Labyrinthe itself out of existence. Theoretically, the site-specificity of the Labyrinthe is gone: 'Si ce dieu [Amour] engage les hommes dans de fâcheux labyrintes, il n'a pas moins le secret de les en tirer lors qu'il est accompagné de la sagesse, dont Aesope dans ses Fables enseigne le chemin' (6). This is the final state of the theory of the Labyrinthe: it is no longer the labyrinth but rather labyrinths. What actually went on in there is another matter. We may never know for sure, and further speculation about it would require a detailed discussion of each one of the thirty-nine fountains, its iconography and sources, and its possible position in and contribution to the heuristics of the Labyrinthe. But some of the complications and possible directions for such a study might be indicated by a brief discussion of the first fountain, 'Le Duc et les Oiseaux'.

Its subject is an owl under hydraulic attack from a great flock of birds [Fig. 15].[46] Perrault remarks that 'le pauvre Duc semble tout honteux de sa disgrace' (*Labyrinte de Versailles*, 8). The texts accompanying the fountain by both Perrault and Benserade make of this an etiological tale. Why does the owl only fly at night? It is because he is ugly and he cannot sing: 'Un jour le Duc fut tellement battu par tous les Oiseaux, à cause de son vilain chant et de son laid plumage, que depuis il n'a osé se montrer que la nuit' ('Le Labyrinthe de Versailles', 242).

The owl is the avian attribute of Minerva, as the peacock is Juno's bird, and the eagle Jupiter's. Its habit of nocturnal hunting is explained in a fable found in the writings of Odo of Chariton: an owl claimed that, as the most beautiful bird, he should have the most beautiful rose. The other birds denied it to him, saying, 'By antiphrasis you are the most beautiful bird, since you are the ugliest.' During the night, however, the owl stole the rose, and in the morning the birds decided that the owl should never again fly in the daytime, nor live with other birds. He would henceforth see better by night, and if he ever again appeared in the light of day, the other birds would attack him.[47]

This first fountain, then, takes up the theory of the Labyrinthe sketched by Perrault's quatrains, and elaborates it. The issue here is 'sagesse', the owl as the attribute of the goddess of wisdom. But that 'sagesse' understood as the prudence of which memory is a part, is both visually ('son laid plumage') and acoustically ('son vilain chant') inappropriate to the daylight world of the new labyrinth. The new labyrinthine experience requires attractive plumage and pleasant song. The new labyrinthine path thus begins with both a reference and a warning: a reference to the ancient wisdom of Minerva's owl, and a warning that that ancient wisdom, specific to the night, is not adequate to the daylight world, 'un jour', of the new labyrinth.

That this reference and its nimbus of association was not lost upon its contemporaries is demonstrated by Cotelle's painting of this first fountain, which shows a group of nymphs and putti engaged in hunting birds with nets [Fig. 13]. In an immensely suggestive study, Pierre Vidal-Naquet has pointed out that, with respect to ancient Athens, it was nocturnal hunting which employed traps and nets, and which was practised by solitary adolescent men and characterized by trickery, *ruse*.[48] This kind of hunting was distinct from the diurnal, collective adult activity which utilized the spear, and whose tactics conformed to the straightforward practices of hand-to-hand combat. The first kind of hunting, further, is practised by the ephebe who has failed to set off, bag his prey and return to take up his proper place in society, as did Theseus. On the contrary, this solitary hunter, whom Vidal-Naquet calls the *chasseur noir*, 'un éphèbe qui, à chaque tournant, a la possibilité d'échouer', resembles Hippolytus. According to some traditions, it was he who invented the net.[49]

One enters the labyrinth, then, positioned as a night hunter, seeking to ensnare night-flying wisdom, only to be met immediately with the impossibility of doing so in this new daylight world, 'un jour'. If the old labyrinth was the setting for the exploits of the successful ephebe, the new Labyrinthe is a place where an entirely different kind of path to success, the path of 'ruse' and 'adresse', must be followed.

The Labyrinthe de Versailles, then, represents a radical replanting of the ancient notion of the labyrinth. In its centrelessness, it forbids the maze-treader the mnemodynamics of departure and return, and, with it, the pure event of the combat. The hero is now to find not the monster but rather himself in a double maze-treading compounded of the *rusé* and the erotic. Meanwhile, the thread of Ariadne has become non-functional, completely powerless as mnemotechnique, and the maze-treader is positioned as a new kind of seeker-after-wisdom, a paradoxical *chasseur noir*. The new experiential topology of the Labyrinthe depends upon the massive forgetting of the story of Theseus and the Minotaur. The new theory of the Labyrinthe, as it was exposed at the entrance to the *bosquet*, and as we may know it from its discursive and iconographic remains, aimed to get the maze-treader through the maze and out the other end by means of a heuristics the methodology of which takes the place of the labyrinthine event. The new labyrinth is the site of a newly formulated process. What it teaches, ultimately, is itself, its own path. It is not the singular and specific setting of a mnemonics, but rather its diffused, pluralized subject. It is to be remembered.

The subject of the last fountain, *Les cannes et le chien*, is a group of large female ducks being pursued around the basin of the fountain by a small hunting dog. As Perrault puts it, the ducks have the word here: 'Elles lui dirent, "Tu te tourmentes en vain, tu as bien assez de force pour nous faire fuir, mais tu n'en as pas assez pour nous prendre"' ('Le Labyrinthe de Versailles', 256–7). Like the first fountain, this last is taken from the writings of Odo of Chariton: a dog tries to defecate on some reeds, but one of them defends itself with a sharp poke, whereupon the dog retreats to a distance and barks. The reed says, 'Better to hear you barking at a distance than to be fouled by you at close quarters.'[50]

This last fountain presents the maze-treader with an elaborate pun. The first punning element involves the reeds (*cannes*) which the fountain produces as female ducks (*cannes*).[51] Also, an alternative name for the 'barbet', the breed of the small water dog chasing the ducks in a circle, is 'canard'.[52] But this fountain has a second, alternative name, and this is Perrault's final comment on it: 'Cette fontaine s'appelle aussi la fontaine du gouffre, parce que les eaux qui entrent dans son bassin avec grande abondance, y tournoient avec rapidité et avec bruit; puis s'engouffrent dans la terre et s'y perdent' (257). Indeed, Le Clerc's engraving shows a whirlpool-like structure, with the three ducks and the *barbet* swimming like little paddle-boats round the basin [Fig. 16]. Scholars have pointed to various kinds of relationship between the garden of Versailles and the anonymous fifteenth-century *Hypnerotomachia Poliphili*. Anthony Blunt saw in Mansart's Colonnade a quotation from one of the book's illustrations, and, most recently, Emanuela Kretzulesco-Quaranta has claimed that the entire garden may be read in terms of the *Songe de Poliphile*.[53] But it seems so far to have escaped notice that this 'gouffre' which is the final fountain in the journey through the Labyrinthe duplicates the labyrinth which is to be found in the French editions of the *Songe*. Starting with the 1546 translation, the woodcut of the labyrinth in the *Songe* was of a unicursal water labyrinth, with little boats whirling around and eventually arriving at the centre [Fig. 17]. It had, that is, exactly the structure of a whirlpool.

So, the ultimate fountain in the Labyrinthe is a memory of a far more traditional labyrinthine topology, a reassertion of centrality, and of the long iconographic tradition of the labyrinth, but with the embellishment of punning word-play on the eternal failure to get the ducks. Having trodden the new maze, and with the exit gate in sight, the maze-treader is presented by the Labyrinthe with an idealized, historicized, but profoundly pessimistic emblem of itself: a souvenir, something by which it might be remembered.

It has escaped almost no one that Racine's *Phèdre*, like the garden of Versailles, has a broad, central spine, whose subject is the renaissance of the King. The precise centre of the play's 1654 lines is marked by lines 827–8, spoken by the nurse Œnone:

> Le Roi, qu'on a cru mort, va paraître à vos yeux;
> Thésée est arrivé, Thésée est en ces lieux.

And the gravity of this structural centre anchors a dizzying series of symmetries—high and low, masculine and feminine, dark and light, sky and earth, mortal and divine, forest and city, age and youth, spirit and body, hunter and hunted, and so on and on—seemingly having the power to inspire endless commentary. But within this delicately yet securely balanced play, Phèdre's declaration scene, with its trip to the labyrinth, is curiously analogous to the Labyrinthe de Versailles, both with respect to its situation and with respect to the experiential topology upon which it depends. The situation of Racine's labyrinth is both inside the play's intricate thematic symmetries, and also outside the play, outside its tragic time, a flashback episode. It is set off from the rest of the tragedy, yet what goes on in there, the avowal of Phèdre's love, is perhaps the play's essential moment, as Roland Barthes has argued.

In its experiential topology, *Phèdre*'s labyrinth is centreless. The monster, the hero's return and the thread are all blurred and redeployed; a new mnemoscape is created in which the labyrinth is finally un-remembered. Similarly, the *bosquet* of the Labyrinthe is centreless, and its topology depends upon a thoroughgoing revision of the notions of the monster and the possibility of return. For the Labyrinthe, the thread itself, and not the loss of memory, is the problem. Finally, we can say that in both the tragic and the horticultural labyrinths, an explicit project of heuristics declares itself:

> C'est moi, Prince, c'est moi dont l'utile secours
> Vous eût du labyrinthe enseigné les détours. (655–6)

I am not arguing for any notion of 'influence', mutual or otherwise, nor am I attempting to document Racine's *Phèdre* or claim that it has a referent in the Labyrinthe de Versailles. Rather, it seems fair to say that both the *bosquet* and the tragedy are engaged in an alternative model of the labyrinthine. It may strike us as curious that Phèdre's expression of her designs upon chastity and innocence should situate itself from within a labyrinth of ethics, a labyrinth in which, as I have noted, the issue is not the issue. But, in a certain way, it is the odd temporal–spatial incommensurability of the labyrinth, in which time and distance are radically disproportionate, which is the issue here. The new, centreless labyrinth makes evident the impossible temporality of memory in general, an impossibility already contained within the definition of memory inherited from Cicero: 'Memoria est per quam animus repetit illa quae fuerunt'; 'Memory is that through which the soul seeks again those [things] which were'. Memory is the site, 'that through which', of compulsive seeking. Actually to find again that which was, as opposed simply to seeking it, is the utopian dream of the project of memory, the equivalent, with respect to imagery, of a return to the garden. We have seen that, in order to gain a history of the centrelessness of both the Labyrinthe of Versailles and the labyrinth of Phèdre's declaration scene, it is necessary to look to a cityscape, the *Labyrinthe royal* of Marie de Médicis' Avignon entry of 1600. This is not historically the first juncture of the project of memory, the labyrinth, and the city. In the second 'Italian Dialogue' of Giordano Bruno, the great Renaissance theoretician of occult memory systems, a small band of potential dinner guests goes astray in the London of the 1580s.[54] Involving an alarming boat ride, treacherous footing and 'much time but little space' (112), the journey's path only brings the travellers back to their point of departure, at which they exclaim, 'O importunate sophisms, O captious cavils, O obscure enigmas, O tangled labyrinths, O enchanted sphinxes—Disentangle yourselves or let yourselves be disentangled' (115).

The urbanization of the centreless labyrinth to be gathered from Bruno's dialogue and from the Avignon entry, the one a labyrinth *in malo*, the other a labyrinth *in bono*, is also far from the last confrontation between memory and the city. The practice of walking in New York occurs, in the formulation of Michel de Certeau, in the 'mobile and endless labyrinths far below' the vantage point of the World Trade Center.[55] It seems, then, that in early modern terms, the project of the centreless labyrinth can be precisely formulated as memorial. Memory seeks again the garden, and finds instead, for the first time, the city. The map of the labyrinthine, centreless, declares the impossibility that memory ever be anything but lost. And it will be precisely in the city, and with respect to the city, and with reference to another fabulous aviary pun, that it will become possible, in two centuries or so, to say that *tout pour moi devient allégorie*. The memorial bestiary will become urban. If Proustian time (memory) begins with Phèdre's 'retrouvée ou perdue', and Baudelairian space (memory) begins with 'Et Phèdre au labyrinthe', then what begins with Phèdre's lost memory, and with the centreless labyrinth of Versailles, is both the ruse and the address of history.

Notes to chapter 3

1. Roland Barthes, *Sur Racine* (Paris: Seuil, 1963), 109–16.
2. Marcel Proust, *Albertine disparue* (Paris: Gallimard, 1989), 43; Leo Spitzer, 'Le "Récit de Théramène"', in *Linguistics and Literary History. Essays in Stylistics* (Princeton: Princeton University Press, 1948), 98.
3. Charles Mauron, *L'Inconscient dans la vie et l'œuvre de Jean Racine* (Aix-en-Provence: La Faculté des lettres, 1957), 164–5. Cf. Penelope Reed Doob, *The Idea of the Labyrinth from Classical Antiquity through the Middle Ages* (Ithaca and London: Cornell University Press, 1990).
4. Francesco Orlando, *Toward a Freudian Theory of Literature—With an Analysis of Racine's Phèdre*, trans. Charmaine Lee (Baltimore and London: Johns Hopkins University Press, 1978), 34.
5. 'Labyrinthe' here refers to the *bosquet* in the garden of Versailles, 'labyrinth' to the general concept.
6. Jean-Marie Apostolidès, *Le Roi-Machine. Spectacle et politique au temps de Louis XIV* (Paris: Minuit, 1981).
7. See Frances Yates, *The Art of Memory* (London: Routledge, 1966).
8. Pierre Nora, 'Entre mémoire et histoire. La Problématique des lieux', in *Les Lieux de mémoire* (Paris: Gallimard, 1984), p. xvii.
9. Maurice Blanchot, *L'Espace littéraire* (Paris: Gallimard, 1955), 234.
10. The connection between *Phèdre* and the Labyrinthe de Versailles has of course not gone entirely unnoticed. See Mme Ronald M. Huebert, 'Racine et le Labyrinthe de Versailles', *Cahiers raciniens* 28 (1970), 19–23; Pierre Han, 'The "Labyrinthe": A Metaphor of Dramatic Action in "Phèdre"', *South Atlantic Bulletin*, 34/4 (1969), 15–17.
11. Euripides, *Hippolytus*, trans. David Grene (Chicago: University of Chicago Press, 1955), 178.
12. For a reading of this midpoint, see Richard E. Goodkin, *The Tragic Middle. Racine, Aristotle, Euripides* (Madison: University of Wisconsin Press, 1991).
13. Charles Segal speculates, however, that Seneca may here be drawing upon Euripides' lost *Hippolytus Veiled*. See his *Language and Desire in Seneca's Phaedra* (Princeton: Princeton University Press, 1986), 121 n. 14.
14. For the Latin text, I have refered to *Seneca's Tragedies*, trans. Frank Justus Miller

(Cambridge, Mass.: Harvard University Press, 1953). English translations are from Seneca, *Three Tragedies*, trans. Frederick Ahl (Ithaca and London: Cornell University Press, 1986), modified.

15. Robert Garnier, *Œuvres complètes* (Paris: Garnier, 1923), i. 239–326.
16. Guérin de La Pinelière, *Hippolyte* (Paris: Antoine de Sommaville, 1635).
17. Gabriel Gilbert, *Hypolite ou le garçon insensible* (Paris: Augustin Courbé, 1647).
18. Mathieu Bidar, *Hippolyte* (Lille: Balthasar Le Francq, 1675).
19. Jacques Pradon, *Phèdre et Hippolyte*, ed. O. Classe (Exeter: University of Exeter, 1987), p. xviii.
20. Ovid, *Metamorphoses*, viii. 158.
21. I have drawn here on the observations of Philippe Borgeaud, 'The Open Entrance to the Closed Palace of the King: The Greek Labyrinth in Context', *History of Religions* 14 (1974), 1–27.
22. The standard monograph on Le Nôtre is F. Hamilton Hazlehurst, *Gardens of Illusion. The Genius of André Le Nostre* (Nashville: Vanderbilt University Press, 1980). On the history of the garden, see Marie Luise Gothein, *Geschichte der Gartenkunst* (1928), 2 vols., trans. Mrs. Archer-Hind (New York: Hacker Art Books, 1979); August Grisebach, *Der Garten. Eine Geschichte seiner Künstlerischen Gestaltung* (Leipzig: Klinhardt & Biermann, [1910]). On the garden in France, see W. H. Adams, *The French Garden 1500–1800* (London: Scholar Press, 1979); Kenneth Woodbridge, *Princely Gardens: The Origins and Development of the French Formal Style* (London: Thames & Hudson, 1986); Denise Le Dantec and Jean-Pierre Le Dantec, *Le Roman des jardins de France: Leur histoire* (Paris: Plon, 1987). For the garden of Versailles in particular, see Hazlehurst, and Robert W. Berger, *In the Garden of the Sun King: Studies on the Park of Versailles under Louis XIV* (Washington: Dumbarton Oaks Research Library and Collection, 1985). Twentieth-cent. sources dealing specifically with the Labyrinthe include the chapter in Alfred Marie, *Naissance de Versailles* (Paris: Vincent Fréal, 1968) i. 121–43, which discusses each fountain and the *Comptes des bâtiments*; Jacques Wilhelm, 'Le Labyrinthe de Versailles', *Revue de l'histoire de Versailles et de Seine-et-Oise*, 38 (1936), 44–63; the chapter in Berger, 'Descriptions of the Labyrinth', 29–40; Michel Conan's postface, 'Les jardins infinis', to Charles Perrault *et al.*, *Labyrinte de Versailles* (1677; Paris: Moniteur, 1982); and Jean Jehasse, 'De la fable aux *Fables*. Benserade et La Fontaine', in *Mélanges offerts à Georges Couton* (Lyon: Presses universitaires de Lyon, 1981), 323–44.
23. Alain-Marie Bassy, 'Les Fables de La Fontaine et le Labyrinthe de Versailles', *Revue d'histoire du livre* 12 (1976), 396–8.
24. Madeleine de Scudéry, *La Promenade de Versailles* (Geneva: Slatkine, 1979), 87.
25. Doob, *The Idea of the Labyrinth*, 112; Marguerite Charageat, 'De la maison Dédalus aux labyrinthes, dans l'art des jardins, du Moyen-Age à la Renaissance', *Actes du XVIIème congrès international d'histoire de l'art, Amsterdam 1952* (The Hague: 1955), 345–50. In addition to the work of Doob cited above, the standard references on the historical and iconographic tradition of the labyrinth are W. H. Mathews, *Mazes and Labyrinths: Their History and Development* (1922; New York: Dover, 1970); Hermann Kern, *Labirinti: Forme e interpretazioni: 5000 anni di presenza di un archetipo*, trans. Libero Sosio (Milan: Feltrinelli, 1981); and Paolo Santarchangeli, *Le Livre des labyrinthes: Histoire d'un mythe et d'un symbole*, trans. Monique Lacau (Paris: Gallimard, 1974).

26. The references to the Labyrinthe in the *Lettres, instructions et mémoires* of Colbert are summarized in Alfred Marie, 140–1.
27. Charles Perrault, 'Le Labyrinthe de Versailles', in *Recueil de divers ouvrages en prose et en vers* (Paris: Jean-Baptiste Coignard, 1675), ed. Jean-Baptiste Collinet, in Charles Perrault, *Contes* (Paris: Gallimard, 1981), 239–57.
28. For a bibliography of editions of the *Manière*, as well as a summary of source criticism concerning it, see Robert W. Berger, 'Review Essay: Manière de montrer les jardins de Versailles', *Journal of Garden History* 4 (1984), 429–31.
29. 'COURROY, signifie aussi de la terre glaise bien battuë & paistrie, qui retient l'eau, & dont on enduit des bassins de fonteines.' Furetière, *Dictionnaire*.
30. Gothein, *Geschichte der Gartenkunst*, ii. 67.
31. The captive, instead of encountering a centre, which at least gave him a certain directionality, now encounters various apparent goals, one after the other; any orientation accordingly becomes impossible.
32. The sense of having entered a constricted world, lacking in law and order, must have been especially strong for the maze-treader who had come from the clear, regular proportions of the park.
33. 'Dans un cabinet de treillage orné d'Architecture, plusieurs Cannes, en tournant avec rapidité au mileu d'un bassin, jettent de l'eau en l'air; & on entend le petit Barbet, qui aboye aprés, en les suivant.' *Labyrinthe de Versailles*, 34.
34. Marc Soriano, *Le Dossier Perrault* (Paris: Hachette, 1972), 167–8. Additional biographical details from the *Contes*, ed. Jean-Pierre Collinet (Paris: Gallimard, 1981). On the role of the *Petite académie*, see Berger, 'Artistic Consultation and Decision-making at Versailles', 7–19.
35. See Berger, 'The Apollo Theme in the Petit Parc', 20–8.
36. Louis XIV, *Manière de montrer les jardins de Versailles* (Paris: Réunion des musées nationaux, 1992), 28.
37. The publication history of Perrault's 'Le Labyrinthe' may reflect this same change of mood. It was included in the 1676 reprinting of his *Recueil*, but was omitted from the reprinting which he supervised in 1701, and which did not appear until 1729.
38. Conan speculates that this may have been because the *bosquet* was more fragile than the rest, and apt to be vandalized. 'Les jardins infinis', unnumbered pages.
39. Conan, 'Les jardins infinis', unnumbered pages.
40. Grisebach, *Der Garten*, Abb. 83.
41. *De inventione, De optimo genere oratorum, Topica*, trans. H. M. Hubbell (London and Cambridge: William Heinemann and Harvard University Press, 1949), ii. 160.
42. See Yates, *The Art of Memory*, ch. 3, 'The Art of Memory in the Middle Ages'.
43. [A. Valadier], 'Le Labyrinthe royal de l'Hercule gaulois triomphant' (Avignon: Jaques Bramereau, 1601).
44. 'Hercules', *Encyclopaedia Britannica*, 11th edn.
45. Hubbell, *De inventione*, supplies 'wisdom'.
46. The association between the owl and the labyrinth is ancient. See Mathews, 45, fig. 29.
47. Ben Edwin Perry (ed.), *Babrius and Phaedrus* (Cambridge: Harvard University Press, 1955), no. 614.

48. Pierre Vidal-Naquet, 'Le Chasseur noir et l'origine de l'éphébie athénienne', in *Le Chasseur noir. Formes de pensées et formes de société dans le monde grec* (Paris: Maspero, 1983), 151–75.
49. Vidal-Naquet, 'Le Chasseur noir', 173. This observation would be the starting point for what Vidal-Naquet calls a 'lecture éphébique' (173 n. 93) of *Phèdre.*
50. Perry (ed.), *Babrius and Phaedrus*, no. 608.
51. 'Cane' and 'canne' were both possible spellings for 'reed'. See Furetière, *Dictionnaire*, s.v. 'cane'.
52. 'Canard se dit aussi d'un chien qui a le poil épais & frisé, qui va à l'eau & qu'on dresse à aller après les canes. On les appelle aussi barbets.' Furetière, *Dictionnaire.*
53. Anthony Blunt, 'The *Hypnerotomachia Poliphili* in 17th-Century France', *Journal of the Warburg Institute* 1 (1937–8), 117–37; Emanuela Kretzulesco-Quaranta, *Les Jardins du songe. 'Poliphile' et la mystique de la renaissance*, 2nd edn. (Paris: Belles Lettres, 1986).
54. *La Cena de le ceneri, The Ash Wednesday Supper*, trans. Edward A. Gosselin and Lawrence S. Lerner (Hamden, CT: Archon Books, 1977).
55. 'Walking in the City', in *The Practice of Everyday Life*, trans. Steven R. Rendall (Berkeley, Los Angeles, London: University of California Press, 1984), 91–110 (92).

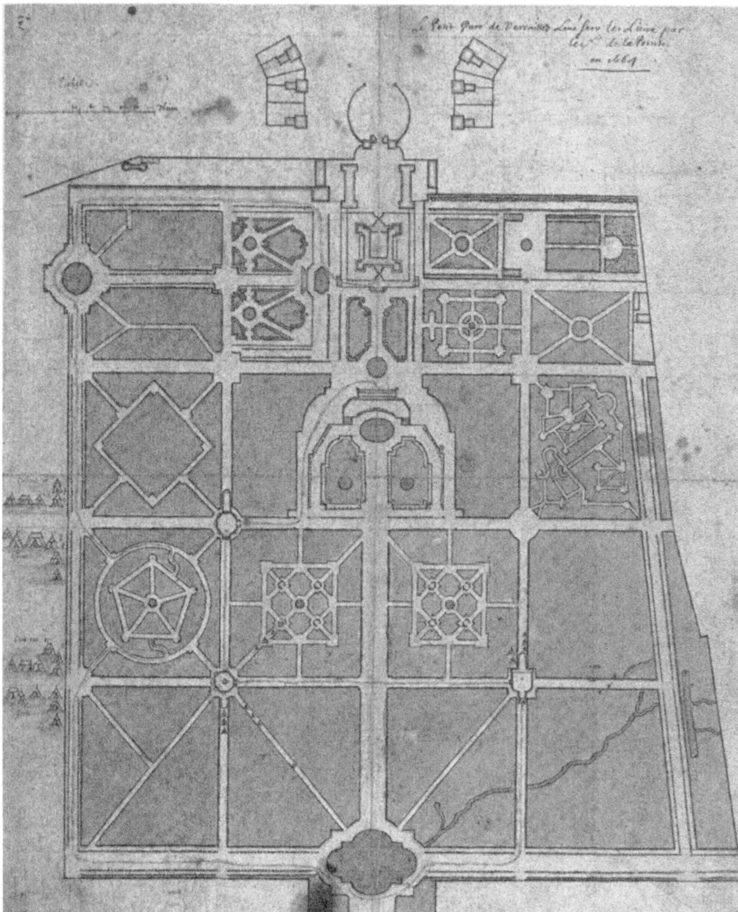

Figure 10. Versailles, plan
Paris: Bibliothèque nationale

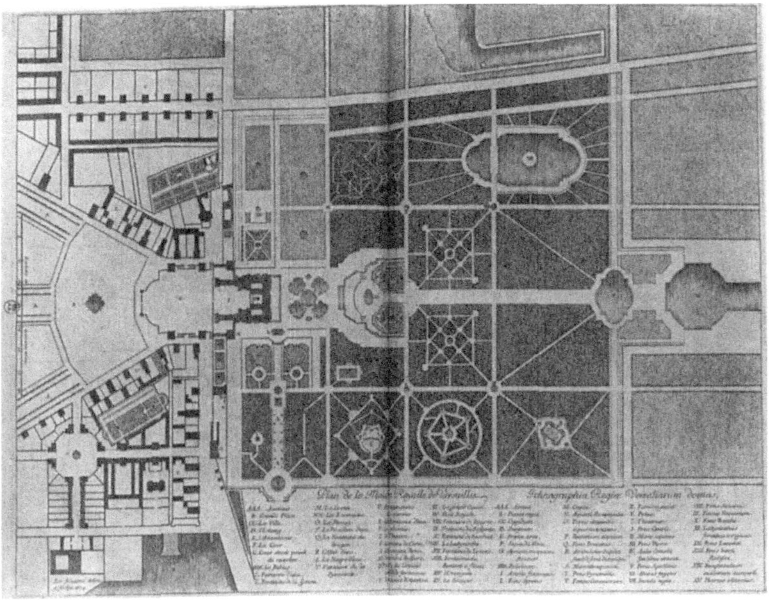

Figure 11. Israel Silvestre
Versailles, plan. Paris: Bibliothèque nationale

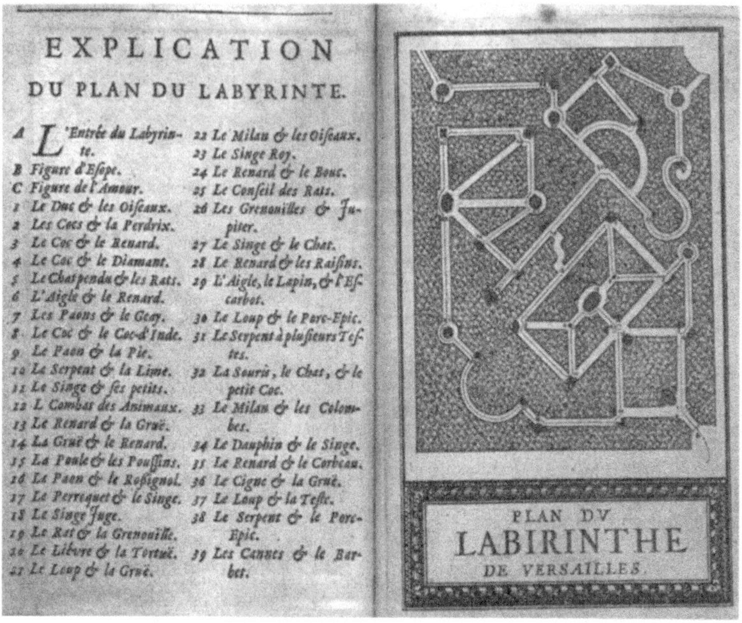

EXPLICATION
DU PLAN DU LABYRINTE.

A L'Entrée du Labyrinte.
B Figure d'Esope.
C Figure de l'Amour.
1 Le Duc & les Oiseaux.
2 Les Cocs & la Perdrix.
3 Le Coc & le Renard.
4 Le Coc & le Diamant.
5 Le Chat pendu & les Rats.
6 L'Aigle & le Renard.
7 Les Paons & le Geay.
8 Le Coc & le Coc-d'Inde.
9 Le Paon & la Pie.
10 Le Serpent & la Lime.
11 Le Singe & ses petits.
12 L Combat des Animaux.
13 Le Renard & la Gruë.
14 La Gruë & le Renard.
15 La Poule & les Poussins.
16 Le Paon & le Rossignol.
17 Le Perroquet & le Singe.
18 Le Singe Juge.
19 Le Rat & la Grenouille.
20 Le Lièvre & la Tortuë.
21 Le Loup & la Gruë.
22 Le Milan & les Oiseaux.
23 Le Singe Roy.
24 Le Renard & le Bouc.
25 Le Conseil des Rats.
26 Les Grenouilles & Jupiter.
27 Le Singe & le Chat.
28 Le Renard & les Raisins.
29 L'Aigle, le Lapin, & l'Escarbot.
30 Le Loup & le Porc-Epic.
31 Le Serpent à plusieurs Testes.
32 La Souris, le Chat, & le petit Coc.
33 Le Milan & les Colombes.
34 Le Dauphin & le Singe.
35 Le Renard & le Corbeau.
36 Le Cigne & la Gruë.
37 Le Loup & la Teste.
38 Le Serpent & le Porc-Epic.
39 Les Cannes & le Barbet.

Figure 12 (above). Sébastien Le Clerc
'Plan du Labirinthe de Versailles' in [Charles Perrault],
Labyrinte de Versailles (Paris: Imprimerie royale, 1679)

Figure 13 (right). Jean Cotelle the Younger
Entrance to the Labyrinth of Versailles. Versailles:
Galerie du Grand Trianon, M.V. 730.

Figure 14. Sébastien Le Clerc
'Esope et l'Amour', in [Charles Perrault],
Labyrinte de Versailles (Paris: Imprimerie royale, 1679)

Figure 15. Sébastien Le Clerc
'Le Duc et les oiseaux', in [Charles Perrault],
Labyrinte de Versailles (Paris: Imprimerie royale, 1679)

Figure 16. Sébastien Le Clerc
'Les cannes et le chien', in [Charles Perrault],
Labyrinte de Versailles (Paris: Imprimerie royale, 1679)

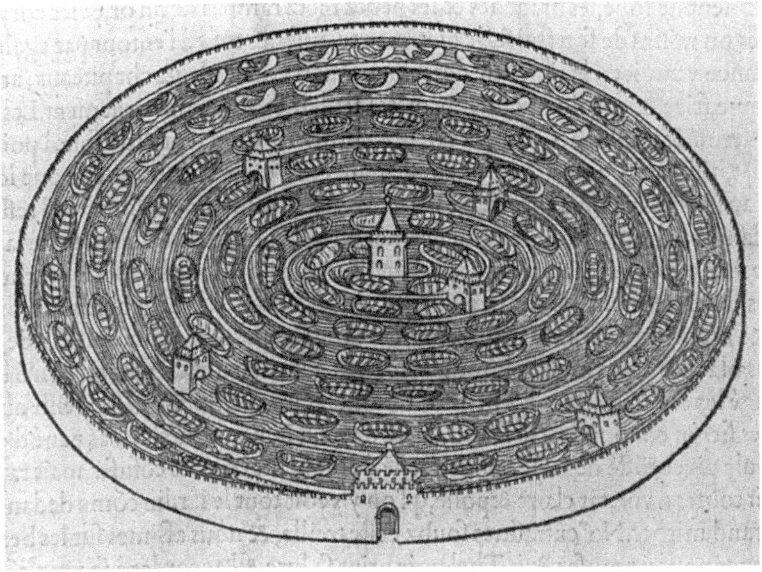

Figure 17. 'Labyrinth', in [Francesco Colonna], *Hypnerotomachie ou Discours du songe de Poliphile*, 2nd edn. (Paris: Iaques Keruer, 1554)

CHAPTER 4

❖

Sublime
Théramène and the Wave

The 'Récit de Théramène', from *Phèdre*'s final act, has been the most frequently criticized passage in the entire Racinian corpus. Starting from the moment of the play's première in 1677, this long narration of the circumstances of the death of Hippolyte, delivered by his governor to a Thésée upon whom it has just begun to dawn that the boy may be innocent, has attracted the attention of readers of Racine. In a discussion published in the same year, and highly critical both of Racine's play and of Pradon's *Phèdre et Hippolyte*, Subligny writes that Racine's *récit* is

> trop long & trop affecté, il n'est pas vray-semblable qu'annonçant à un père la mort de son fils, on s'amuse à faire la description des beaux chevaux qui l'ont tué, qu'on frise jusqu'au moindre de leurs crins, qu'on marque toutes leurs démarches, qu'on leur fasse mesme de chagrin baisser la teste & les oreilles, comme des rosses, & qu'on fasse la peinture de leurs harnois, jusqu'à leurs reins flottantes.[1]

It was not just the horses that bothered Subligny. After borrowing from Horace a highly resonant image which allowed him to compare the *récit* to a beautiful cypress tree which a painter with bad judgement has placed in the middle of a stormy seascape, Subligny arrived at the issue in terms of which the critical discussion of the *récit* was subsequently framed: the eloquence of the description of the water.

> Cependant, sur le dos de la plaine liquide,
> S'éleve à gros boüillons une montagne humide.
>
> Les belles Phrases Poëtiques, que les Ecoliers doivent trouver cela charmant, ces deux Vers meritent un prix dans la plus forte Rethorique, *le dos de la plaine liquide*, pour dire sur la mer ou sur l'eau, *une montagne qui s'éleve à gros boüillons*, cela est nouveau. (55–6)

Subligny proceeds to note that the present mountain, if it is indeed of water, cannot reasonably be called 'humide', just as water in general cannot be said to be damp. Also, he wishes to point out the oddity of Racine's claim that Hippolyte, a prince after all, has personally tended to his horses. The final straw is the line, 'Un Dieu, qui d'aiguillons pressoit leurs flancs poudreux'. As for himself, Subligny concludes, 'je ne puis souffrir que Monsieur Racine fasse un Dieu Piqueboeuf, & un Prince Palfrenier' (56).

Subligny's comments, with the accusation of schoolboy rhetoric placing them firmly within the seventeenth-century critique of hyperbole,[2] seem to have called forth no explicit response from Racine and his vigilant friend Boileau. Rather, the two, who found themselves in the early months of 1677 engaged in the high-stakes battle known as 'La Querelle des deux *Phèdres*',[3] seemed to feel that Subligny could be safely disregarded. Exactly thirty years later, however, when Racine was dead and Boileau was ailing, a critical commentary of the *récit de Théramène* by Antoine Houdart de La Motte provoked an explicit rejoinder from Boileau from beyond the grave.

Houdart de La Motte (1672–1731) was the successor to Thomas Corneille in the Académie française (1709). His collected works run to ten volumes in the edition of 1754; and, when a selection of his writings was republished in 1859 as *Les Paradoxes littéraires*, his editor asserted that at least one of his essays was 'justement citée comme un modèle, et mérite d'être étudiée sous ce rapport par tous ceux qui tiennent à conserver intact le dépôt de la vraie politesse française'.[4] La Motte's place in the history of eighteenth-century literary discourse was secured by his arguments in favor of prose theatre. He had written his own tragedy of *Œdipe* first in prose, and only subsequently in verse, and he argued, in the 1726 'Discours à l'occasion de la tragédie d'Œdipe', that prose tragedy is at least as poetic as verse tragedy. He went so far as to cast the first scene of Racine's *Mithridate* into prose and publish it, claiming that it was in no way inferior to the version in verse.

La Motte's criticism of the *récit de Théramène* first appeared in 1707, in a 'Discours sur la poésie en général et sur l'Ode en particulier', which was published at the head of his *Odes*.[5] While Subligny's critique had referred to the problem of the 'vray-semblable', La Motte framed the problem in terms of genre, voice and poetic fury. Where Subligny's critical terms for the *récit* had been 'trop long & trop affecté', what La Motte heard was the swollen ('l'enflure') and the excessive ('l'excès de l'expression'). The genre-specific argument was bound up with the problem of the voice. There is, writes La Motte, an 'hardiesse de langage' which characterizes the ode, and which it has in common only with the epic poem, 'lorsqu'il ne fait pas parler ses personnages. Le poëte y est poëte de profession, au lieu que dans les autres ouvrages, il emprunte, pour ainsi dire, un esprit & des sentimens étrangers; & il doit se contenter alors de toute l'élégance du langage ordinaire, sans y laisser sentir d'étude ni d'affection' (88). The professed voice of the poet is thus to be distinguished from ordinary language, which has nevertheless its own elegance. Tragic poets must not allow their own authorial voices to be heard:

> Les poëtes tragiques même, qui s'abandonnent quelquefois à l'enflure, doivent toujours être en garde contre l'excès de l'expression. Comme ils ne font point parler des poëtes, mais des hommes ordinaires, ils ne doivent qu'exprimer les sentiments qui conviennent à leurs acteurs, et prendre pour cela les tours et les termes que la passion offre le plus naturellement. Racine n'a presque jamais passé ces bornes, que dans quelques descriptions où il a affecté d'être poëte: comme dans celle de la mort d'Hippolyte, où l'on croit plutôt entendre l'auteur que le personnage qu'il fait parler. (88)

For La Motte, then, genre determines not only whose voice shall be heard, but also whether that voice shall speak with poetic richness or with naturally offered terms and turns. But lyric poets are required to speak differently from the common run of men:

> Mais les poëtes lyriques, j'entends les auteurs d'odes, peuvent et doivent même étaler les richesses de la poésie. Ils peuvent, sans nuire néanmoins à la clarté, parler autrement que le commun des hommes; et pourvu que le sens soit fort, et que les images soient vives, à proportion de la hardiesse du langage, ils auront d'autant plus atteint la perfection de leur art, qu'ils auront plus heureusement hasardé. (89)

The series of distinctions which La Motte is making does not originate with him. One thinks immediately of the third book of the *Republic*, and its distinction between 'simple narration', when Homer speaks 'just as Homer', and its opposite, 'imitation', 'when one takes away from the poet all the parts between the speeches, and leaves only the interchange of talk' (394). Based on this distinction, 'poetry and fabling are of two kinds: one wholly through imitation, as you say, tragedy and comedy; the other through the poet's own report of things. You would find this best in the dithyramb. A third kind, using both, is in epic poetry, and in many other places too' (394c). This distinction is followed in the third chapter of Aristotle's *Poetics*, and in Chapter 24, where Homer is praised 'because he alone realizes when he should write in his own person. A poet should himself say very little, for he is not then engaged in imitation.' But, in spite of the fact that La Motte is working with established distinctions, finding authorization for his own voice in his own lyric poetry, where Plato had established it for the lyric genre of the dithyramb, La Motte's nineteenth-century posterity pointed specifically to this discussion as inaugural. 'Toute cette discussion est un chef-d'œuvre,' wrote his editor in 1859, 'ces différences, en quelque sorte *morales*, que Lamotte signalait le premier, entre le poëte lyrique, le poëte épique et le poëte dramatique, sont aujourd'hui admises par tous les littérateurs, qui ne font pas toujours honneur de cette belle division à celui qui l'a trouvée' (89, note 1). It was within this discussion of genres and voices, which seems quite tame, but was nevertheless perceived by readers of La Motte to be determining, that the eloquence expended by Racine upon the sea once again, after thirty years, became pertinent. Whereas Subligny had scorned the humidity of the mountain of water, it was the wave's motion which was singled out by La Motte, in the one Alexandrine which then occupied Racinian criticism for the next fifty years:

> Ce vers de Racine:
>
> Le flot qui l'apporta, recule épouvanté,
>
> est excessif dans la bouche de Théramène. On est choqué de voir un homme accablé de douleur, si recherché dans ses termes, et si attentif à sa description. Mais ce même vers serait beau dans une ode, parce que c'est le poëte qui y parle, qu'il y fait profession de peindre, qu'on lui suppose point de passion violente qui partage son attention, et qu'on sent bien enfin, quand il se sert d'une expression outrée, qu'il le fait à dessein, pour suppléer par l'exagération de l'image, à l'absence de la chose même. (89)

This charge then leads La Motte into a discussion of poetic fury, and it is a discussion which justifies the nineteenth-century title given to his writings: *Les Paradoxes littéraires*. For his observation is, 'Enthousiasme tant qu'on voudra, il faut qu'il soit toujours guidé par la raison, et que le poëte le plus échauffé se rappelle souvent à soi, pour juger sainement de ce que son imagination lui offre' (90). In Théramène's mouth, then, the line about the wave is wrong not only because it mixes up two things which ought to be kept separate, causing a moment of lyric poetry to intrude into the tragedy, but also because, paradoxically, the very strength of the image betrays the heated inspiration of the poet, and not a moment of passion expressed in the ordinary language of the common man.

If 'chef-d'œuvre' seems today to be somewhat unlikely praise for La Motte's argument, if it points up a certain distance separating us from the critical concerns of the mid-nineteenth century, then the eighteenth-century uproar over this wave, initiated by La Motte's quotation of Racine's line, is even more difficult to imagine. But perhaps it is best not to begin by underestimating La Motte. After all, Boileau, who had managed simply to assimilate Subligny's critique to his general defence of Racine against Pradon, saw fit specifically to take up La Motte's charge. Indeed, as Mesnard remarked in the Grands Ecrivains edition of Racine, Boileau seems to have sensed 'le danger de cette critique, qui pouvait mener loin et jusqu'à une poétique nouvelle'.[6] So, after Boileau's death in 1711, there appeared his response to La Motte in the eleventh and twelfth *Réflexions critiques* (1713).[7] Not to be outdone by this voice from beyond the grave, La Motte in the same year published a response to Boileau,[8] after which Fénelon, joining the discussion on the side of La Motte, claimed in the 'Lettre à l'Académie' that the entire *récit* could and should be reduced to, 'Hippolyte est mort. Un monstre envoyé du fonds de la mer par la colère des dieux l'a fait périr. Je l'ai vu.'[9]

Meanwhile, Racine's youngest son, Louis, had been growing up. On 3 December 1728, he delivered to the Académie des inscriptions a 'Comparaison de l'Hipolyte d'Euripide avec la tragédie de Racine sur le même sujet', which was published in 1752 along with his *Remarques sur les tragédies de Jean Racine.*[10] By this time, it was apparently possible to claim that Théramène's speech was precisely *vraisemblable*, composed exactly of the terms and turns naturally offered by passion:

> Quant à Théramène, je ne crois pas non plus qu'il soit impossible de le défendre. En entrant sur le théâtre, il s'est écrié d'abord: 'Hippolyte n'est plus!' Par ces mots rapides il a annoncé toute la nouvelle, et satisfait aux premiers mouvemens de sa douleur. Il a maintenant repris ses esprits, il est en état de raconter le détail de cette mort; et comme il est frappé de toutes les circonstances d'une aventure si cruelle, il les raconte avec la même passion que s'il les voyoit encore: l'affroi dont il est pénétré lui fait employer les images les plus vives; il croit voir encore le monstre sortir des flots. (130)

In 1728, Louis seemed to feel that his reading was responsive to the critical history of the *récit*: 'De telles raisons balanceroient peut-être les critiques qu'on a faites de ce fameux récit' (131). But, by the time he published additional comments on this passage in the 1752 *Remarques*, the situation seemed to be out of hand, and it had become impossible to respond adequately: 'On a tant écrit de choses sur ce fameux récit, que j'en ai peu à dire: je ferois un commentaire trop long et trop ennuyeux, si je voulois répondre à toutes les critiques, si je voulois seulement les rapporter' (194). At this point, Louis can but repeat his assertion from 1728 in more explicit terms, claiming for the language of Théramène exactly that status which La Motte had denied it, the status of ordinary language: 'Ce qu'on veut appeler style poétique et pompeux est, pour ceux qui connoissent la nature, le langage ordinaire de la vive douleur' (194–5).

What, we might wonder, happened between about 1728 and about 1752 to turn a situation which Louis Racine, who considered himself to be the keeper of the family flame, had earlier perceived as capable of being balanced, into one which seemed to be out of control? The short answer to this question is that his father had become classic. The same readers who had chosen the *récit de Théramène* as a critical battleground, and had made the wave into the battlefield of the discussion, had at the same time invented the modern literary canon in France, and they had performed this move in terms of the classic. The Racinian text exists at the crossroads of this event. All entangled are the readings of the *récit de Théramène*, the modalities of canon establishment, and the will to label it 'classic'. By separating out these strands, the literary canon, here at one of its earliest moments in France, can be seen as a series of acts of memory conditioned by the nostalgic in general. Another way in which to formulate the problem which was bothering Louis Racine in 1752 might be to say that his father was no longer Racine, but rather had become 'Racine', by which I mean to designate that Racinian text which has undergone a nostalgic labelling. This nostalgic processing will be read, in what follows, at the level of Racine's language itself, and in the three contributions which led Louis Racine to perceive the situation as having escaped him. The wave of the *récit de Théramène* is a prominent issue in each, and they all appeared in 1738: the *Remarques de grammaire sur Racine*, by the abbé d'Olivet; Desfontaines's *Racine vengé*; and the *Observations critiques à l'occasion des Remarques de grammaire sur Racine*, by Jean Soubeiran de Scopon. Finally, Boileau's reply to La Motte in

1713 will be read for its contribution to the possibility for the construction of 'Racine'.

If one consults a seventeenth-century dictionary for the definition of the adjective 'classique', one finds but a single connotation: 'classique' applies to what is read, or what holds great authority, in classes. 'Qui ne se dit guerres que des Auteurs qu'on lit dans les classes, dans les escoles, ou qui y ont grande autorité', Furetière's dictionary begins. Examples of classic authors are St Thomas, Aristotle, Cicero and Virgil. However, by the mid-eighteenth century, and the appearance of the entry 'classique' in the *Encyclopédie* of Diderot and d'Alembert, a coda had been added to the definitions of the word which had begun to accumulate. The first meaning of the word is still that of Furetière's definition: '[l]es auteurs que l'on explique dans les collèges'. But the entry continues,

> On peut dans ce dernier sens donner le nom d'auteurs *classiques François* aux bons auteurs du siecle de Louis XIV, & de celui-ci; mais on doit plus particulierement appliquer le nom de *classiques* aux auteurs qui ont écrit tout à la fois élégamment & correctement, tels que Despréaux, Racine, &c. Il serait à souhaiter, comme le remarque M. de Voltaire, que l'académie Françoise donnât une édition correcte des auteurs *classiques* avec des remarques de Grammaire.

On 10 April 1761 Voltaire wrote from Ferney two letters which mentioned this project of edition and codification. One, to Charles Pinot Duclos, greeted the news that the Academy had undertaken to produce a series of editions of 'nos auteurs classiques': 'Je vous assure monsieur, que vous me faites grand plaisir en m'apprenant que l'Académie va rendre à la France et à l'Europe le service de publier un recueil de nos auteurs classiques avec des notes qui fixeront la langue et le goût, deux choses assez inconstantes dans ma volage patrie.'[11] The edition of classic authors is thus, for Voltaire, the occasion for the writing of notes which will fix both language and taste. Both lack constancy, and the French classics are to be produced in order to conform two things which are flighty.

Voltaire's comments participate in a history of the desire for fixity in language, which would itself be a chapter in a much broader history of the suspicion of change and changeability. This is a broad and complex cultural stance, as appears when we recall that the Academy of Painting and Sculpture looked askance at the valorization of colour during the debates of the 1660s and 70s, because colour depends upon light and changes with it. However, the tension between change and fixity had been a general characteristic of the project of the French language for some considerable time prior to Voltaire's advocacy of the fixation of the language. Vaugelas's preface to the *Remarques*, for example, notes, 'C'est la destinée de toutes les langues vivantes d'estre sujetes au changement. [...] Si l'on avoit esgard à ce changement, en vain on travailleroit aux Grammaires & aux Dictionnaires des Langues vivantes.'[12] The Academy's preface to the first edition of its Dictionary in 1694 holds that 'If there has ever been the promise that a living Language may come to be fixed, and no longer to depend on the caprice and the tyranny of Usage, we have reason to believe that ours has reached in our days to that glorious point of immutability'.[13] The desire to fix taste also has a long and complex history, the seventeenth-century French chapter of which has been written.[14] The notion of the author as the paragon which will stand against flights of fancy in language is also an old one by Voltaire's time. Along with the usage of the court, Vaugelas had recommended 'la façon d'escrire de la plus saine partie des Autheurs du temps' (Preface, unnumbered pages) as definitive of good usage. And the statutes of the Academy had included a directive that the Academicians should examine 'les meilleurs auteurs de la langue françoise'.

But what is the specificity of the will to label this activity, one tool in a vast cultural construction project, 'classic'? The other letter written that day from Ferney was even more explicit about the uses to which the classic would be put. From it, we learn that the idea for the project of the classic was not originally Voltaire's. The letter is addressed to Pierre-Joseph Thoulier d'Olivet, abbé, member of the Academy and co-editor of the *Tusculan Disputations* of Cicero: 'Eh bien voilà votre ancien projet de donner un receuil d'auteurs classiques, qui fait fortune. Rien ne sera plus glorieux pour l'académie, ny plus utile pour les Français et pour les étrangers. Il est temps de prévenir (j'ay presque dit d'arrèter) la décadence de la langue et du goust.'[15] The classic here stands explicitly against decadence in language and taste, whether that decadence be yet to come or already at hand. The idea was d'Olivet's, and it was, by this time, an old one: 'votre ancien projet'. In fact—has Voltaire forgotten it? There is no mention of it in his 1761 letter—d'Olivet had already begun to publish his project. It had been in 1738; the book was his *Remarques de grammaire sur Racine* (Paris: Gandouin).

The abbé d'Olivet (1682–1768) was an erudite humanist.[16] He railed against the café society of his day ('Les cafés ont perverti absolument le goût'),[17] and hated in particular his two fellow academicians Marivaux and Montesquieu, 'ce fou'.[18] Sent to Paris as a young man to study theology, he had met the ageing Boileau, and this appears to have been the deciding incident in his life. His ambition was to become a new Boileau, defending beautiful language in an era which he felt intensely to be one of decadence. He became a Jesuit and was sent to Rome in 1713 to continue the history of the Society begun by Jouvancy. Whatever happened in Rome, we know that he left the Society. His *Discours de réception* in the Academy contains vigorous remarks on the causes of the decadence of taste. In this, d'Olivet was one of many who sensed standards to be generally in decline.[19] But his was a particularly prominent voice on this theme: the opponents of the philosophes in the Academy of the 1760s were called *les d'Olivets*.[20]

D'Olivet seems to have spent the 1720s preparing his first edition of Cicero, and conducting a love affair, while awaiting the death of the woman's rich husband. But the affair ended badly: in the early days of November 1730,[21] d'Olivet returned from an extended trip to Holland only to find that the woman, from whom he had received a letter in Lille only five days previously, had died, but only that day: 'Il arrive, il court chez elle, il la trouve morte depuis trois heures.'[22]

The structure of this event in d'Olivet's life is noteworthy: firstly, a seemingly unproblematic return is effected, but it is a return to something which is literally and shockingly already dead. The object of the return is a body which is a corpse, but only just. Further, it is a body which was never fully known in the first place, for the woman so lately dead, 'à l'âge de vingt ans, [...] accoucha si douloureusement, et avec tant de danger, que depuis elle ne s'est point exposée à avoir des enfants' (i. 159–60). Finally, the structure of departure and return to the surprisingly dead is ruled over by the sentiment of inevitable decline and decadence: the pair, it seems, were expecting her rich, 73-year-old husband to die presently, and then to enjoy his money. She was already, in d'Olivet's prose, 'la veuve': 'Notre ami était philosophe à bon marché, prévoyant d'un jour à l'autre la mort du mari, et un revenu qui était plus pour lui que pour la veuve' (i. 159–60).

There was no abatement in d'Olivet's problems with women, and, at the end of 1733, his involvement with Racine became curiously conflated with them. The lieutenant of police received a denunciation of d'Olivet, who, it seems, had been receiving treatment for syphilis, had been flaunting a mistress, and had stolen one of Racine's manuscripts from his sons, and sold it to a publisher:

> M. l'abbé d'Olivet [...] prétexta, il y a dix-huit mois, un voyage en province, et se mit à Paris entre les mains d'un homme qui travailla longtemps à lui purifier le sang.
>
> Il est si entêté d'une femme, qu'il la promène partout, et quoique prêtre, il ne rougit point de se montrer à côté d'elle dans les spectacles. [...]
>
> En travaillant à l'histoire de l'Académie française, il demanda à MM. Racine des éclaircissements sur la vie de leur père. On lui communiqua plusieurs papiers, parmi lesquels il trouva un manuscrit de ce fameux auteur, qu'il vendit à un libraire qui le fit imprimer.[23]

So, in the first half of the 1730s, d'Olivet was not having an easy time of it. His long-term love affair ended cataclysmically, and took on almost allegorical dimensions in his re-telling of it to his correspondant Bouhier; he was allegedly ill, certainly in trouble with the authorities, and next to these problems stands a purloined manuscript—of Racine. What happened next is that, from within these structures, d'Olivet produced the version of the French classic which has since become standard.

By the end of December 1737, d'Olivet was able to write to Bouhier, 'Ma vie est la plus unie du monde. J'aime mes livres plus que jamais, et je suis même parvenu à n'aimer que mes livres. Il y a cinq ans que je me suis défendu absolument de souper dehors, et j'y dîne rarement. Du reste, nulle sorte de passion.'[24] This is the first instance of the construction in question: the hapless love of the abbé d'Olivet is explicitly transferred onto books. And, since the work of translation cannot be sustained, some little diversion is necessary: 'Comme la traduction me dégoûte à la longue, je me permets souvent de petites diversions. Par exemple, je viens de faire des notes de grammaire sur les tragédies de Racine.' The work to which he is referring is the *Remarques de grammaire sur Racine*, which appeared in the next year, and which declared Racine to be classic.

But, just as Voltaire had attributed the responsibility for collecting classic authors to d'Olivet, so d'Olivet places the origin of the project elsewhere. 'Pour annoncer d'abord mon dessein,' he begins the introduction to his *Remarques*, 'il me suffira de rappeler ici une idée de M. Despréaux.' Boileau's idea, however, was not to create the

French classic from the French but to establish the classic on the ground of translation. D'Olivet quotes him at length:

'Je voudrais, disait-il, que la France pût avoir ses Auteurs classiques, aussi-bien que l'Italie. Pour cela, il nous faudroit un certain nombre de livres, qui fussent déclarez exempts de fautes, quant au style. Quel est le Tribunal qui aura droit de prononcer là-dessus, si ce n'est l'Académie? Je voudrais qu'elle prît d'abord le peu que nous avons de bonnes Traductions; qu'elle invitât ceux qui ont ce talent, à en faire de nouvelles; & que si elle ne jugoit pas à propos de corriger tout, ce qu'elle y trouveroit d'équivoque, d'hasardé, de négligé, elle fût au moins exacte à le marquer au bas des pages, dans une espèce de commentaire, qui ne fût que grammaticale. (3)

Boileau's project for the 'French' classic, then, was the making-French of the authors of classical antiquity.[25] The intersection between the Racinian text and this project occurs when the abbé d'Olivet does to Boileau precisely what Boileau had done to Longinus in the 1701 preface to his *Œuvres complètes*: he takes over and moves in to his critical structure, but he makes it French, sweeping aside the issue of translation.

More than a quarter century after the appearance of his translation of the *On the Sublime* in 1674, Boileau published the first edition of his collected works which bore his name. One of the projects of the preface to his 1701 edition is the re-exemplification of the Longinian text. The reply of Alexander to his minister Parmenion upon being offered half of Asia and his daughter in marriage by Darius ('Pour moy,' luy disoit Parmenion, 'si j'estois Alexandre j'accepterois ces offres.' 'Et moy aussi,' répliqua ce Prince, 'si j'estois Parmenion.')[26] is more than translated by Boileau. The 1701 preface transports this example of 'la Sublimité dans les pensées' to the history of France, and to the reply of a French prince, Louis XII, to his ministers:

Considérons, par exemple, cette réplique si fameuse de Louis douzième à ceux de ses ministres qui lui conseillaient de faire punir plusieurs personnes qui, sous le règne précédent, et lorsqu'il n'était encore que duc d'Orléans, avaient pris à tâche de le desservir. 'Un roi de France, leur répondit-il, ne venge point les injures d'un duc d'Orléans.'[27]

As an example of what he calls 'extravagance', Boileau cites two lines from the final scene of Théophile de Viau's *Pyrame et Thisbé*:

Ah! voici le poignard qui du sang de son maître
S'est souillé lâchement. Il en rougit, le traître!

Toutes les glaces du Nord ensemble ne sont pas, à mon sens plus froides que cette pensée. Quelle extravagance, bon Dieu! de vouloir que la rougeur de sang dont est teint le poignard d'un homme qui vient de s'en tuer lui-même soit un effet de la honte qu'a ce poignard de l'avoir tué! (50)

The ice and chill of this critical vocabulary, as well as the procedure of criticizing by exclamation and not by argument, come from the chapter of the *Traité du Sublime* for which Boileau himself supplied the title 'Du Stile froid'.[28] It contains this language, translating the criticism of a kind of punning on the part of Xenophon: 'C'estoit à Amphicrate et non pas à Xenophon d'appeller les prunelles des Vierges pleines de pudeur. Quelle pensée! bon Dieu! parce que le mot de *Coré* qui signifie en Grec la prunelle de l'oeil, signifie aussi une vierge, de vouloir que toutes les prunelles universellement soient des vierges pleines de modestie' (55). In transporting the Longinian example to France, and in rewriting it, Boileau has deflected the focus of the criticism. The exclamatory moment in the Longinian text has been produced in response to a pun, a metonymic play of association on the Greek word for the pupil of the eye, which may also mean 'virgin'. The lines of Théophile quoted by Boileau, however, have nothing to do with this problem. Rather, they exemplify the conceit of attributing passion to lifeless objects and animals by an analogy of effects, which Boileau calls, in the *Réflexion critique XI*, 'hyperbole'. In making the 'stile froid' French, Boileau has not given a symmetrical example. Its critical index is no longer metonymic but metaphoric. And this is not just any metaphor. It is precisely the procedure followed by the wave of the *récit de Théramène*, which Boileau staunchly defended.

Further, the new example of 'la sublimité dans les pensées' is no more symmetrical with the old than is the new example of the 'style froid'. In his transfer of the *bon mot* of the monarch, Boileau has eliminated the problem of the counsellor. Alexander's distinction, in the example from Longinus, is to be not Parmenion, not a minister. The distinction of Louis XII in the new example, is to be not exactly himself. He calls himself not 'Louis XII', but 'un roi de France'. As such, occupying the absolute position of 'roi', he is most importantly not that which is closest to him: his own past self, 'un Duc d'Orléans'. The problem of the minister is swept aside in the face of the becoming-absolute of a king of France. In so far as it had been problems of translation which occupied Boileau's preface to his 1674

Longinus, we can observe that, in allegorical terms, he has succeeded in eliminating that problem in the 1701 preface. The minister, that mediating, translating element between monarchs, has been edged out of his position. The originating language is French and it is itself; it is absolute and most importantly not any other language. That it is not a translation is, by 1701, self-evident.

What is important about these moves on Boileau's part is not their substance but their procedure. The project of domesticating Longinus, of first translating and then transporting and re-exemplifying the Longinian text, has led to the transformation of the critical concerns of the original, all the while, however, retaining its forms and terms. By 1701, there was a French sublime, but it was inaugural.

By 1738, there was a French classic, but it too was inaugural. As recently as 1729, in his continuation of Pellisson's *Histoire de l'Académie française*, d'Olivet had been able to write, concerning the problem of exemplarity in the *Dictionnaire*, 'Mais avant qu'elle commençât son vocabulaire, l'Italie avoit des auteurs reconnus pour classiques, et nous n'en avons point encore de tels.'[29]

Encore? After quoting Boileau on the establishment of the French classic on the basis of translations, d'Olivet in the preface to the 1738 *Remarques* first approves of what he calls Boileau's 'idée solide'. However, he then moves in to this solid idea and takes over its structure while deflecting its focus and transforming its content. D'Olivet's gesture is magisterial. He simply objects to basing the project of the French classic on translation, and asserts that he would rather base it on 'ceux de nos ouvrages François, dont le mérite, depuis cinquante ou soixante ans, est avoué de tout le monde. Car enfin, toute prévention à part, il me semble que la langue Françoise a des Auteurs, qui peuvent également servir de modèles, & pour bien penser, & pour bien écrire' (5). D'Olivet decides that Boileau's project should avail itself of Boileau's poetry, and Racine's: 'Je crois ne pouvoir mieux seconder les vûes de M. Despréaux, qu'en m'attachant à ses Poësies, & à celles de M. Racine; persuadé comme je suis avec toute la France, qu'ils mériteroient incontestablement d'être mis à la tête de nos Auteurs classiques' (5–6). D'Olivet thus appropriates Boileau's critical structure, the establishment of the French classic, but entirely transforms its content. In this, he duplicates the gesture of Boileau's 1701 preface. There, the structure of the Longinian sublime had been retained, but its content transformed. Further, as d'Olivet evidently sees clearly, the problem which must be eliminated in this case is also that of translation. Just as Boileau had both allegorically and effectively eliminated translation in making the sublime French, so here it is the translated which d'Olivet eliminates in making the classic French. The French classic will be based upon French poetry and not upon French prose translations, and we might ask now what modalities of reading allowed the Racinian text to fall under this label.

I said by way of introduction that, of all the passages of *Phèdre*, it is the *récit de Théramène* which has most generally been perceived not to fit. Within this passage, the major irritant has been the wave: 'Le flot qui l'apporta, recule épouvanté'. D'Olivet's location of the French classic in Racine, and his language having to do with homogeneity, 'avoué de tout le monde', 'avec toute la France', 'incontestablement', must thus contend with this wave.[30] It must be reclaimed for a critical vocabulary which denies the excessive.

D'Olivet's recuperation of the wave goes to two points: 'quel est le langage ordinaire de la poësie, & quelle a été l'origine de ce langage' (33). As to the first point, d'Olivet asserts, following comments of Boileau in the eleventh *Réflexion critique* and in the *Art poëtique*, that there is an ordinary language which is native to poetry, and, in that language, 'il n'y a point de figure plus ordinaire [...] que de personnifier les choses inanimées' (33). For 'les Physiciens', says d'Olivet, a wave is a certain quantity of water. But, for poets, 'ce sera un individu animé, un être pensant, & même, s'ils en ont envie, ce sera une divinité' (33).

The difficulty with this argument, however, is that, in following the critical programme of Boileau, it must necessarily pass over in silence the one text which is both chronologically and ideologically central to that programme. D'Olivet finds authorization for this first point in Boileau's *Art poëtique*, from 1674, and in the eleventh *Réflexion critique*, from 1713. Both texts do indeed defend the attribution of passion to the sea. However, in the middle of these texts stands the 1701 preface to Boileau's collected works. D'Olivet follows the critical movement of this particular text, the re-exemplification of the sublime, in establishing the French classic. However, Boileau's French sublime is established in opposition to the attributing of passion to lifeless objects, in this case, the sword of Pyramus. In order to use Boileau as a reference, d'Olivet is forced to look away from the one text which has established his own critical methodology.

This problem seems not have been sensed in explicit terms by d'Olivet's contemporaries.[31] His second point of defence of the wave, however, provoked a great hue and cry. D'Olivet proceeded to claim that Racine's project in having Théramène attribute passions to the sea was a historicist one. Théramène lived, he says, in a time and place in which physical science 'reconnoissoit une ame répandue dans tout ce qui éxiste' (34). This doctrine is attributable to 'Moschus, Phénicien', and, if it is admitted into the discussion, then poetry becomes nothing other than the expression of a particular view of the natural world: 'Ainsi le langage de la Poësie, fut originairement le langage de la Phisique, ou du moins ne fut qu'une conséquence & une extention des idées généralement reçues par les plus célébres Physiciens' (35). This observation allows d'Olivet to claim that poetry is the steady, unmoving, dependable index into the view of the natural world which existed at the time of Homer, while science and its language comes and goes:

> Plus de trois mille ans se sont écoulés, depuis que la Physique forma le langage de la Poësie; & quand la Physique a changé d'opinion, ce qui lui est arrivé depuis tant de siécles une infinité de fois, en même-temps elle a toujours changé son langage; mais au contraire, la Poësie a toujours retenu le sien, parce qu'en effet le sistême de l'ancienne Physique est le seul qui autorise la fiction. (35)

D'Olivet's historicism thus produces an argument which reverses the problem of the wave. He stabilizes the language of the wave as the language of poetry itself. This is a forceful moment within the general project of the establishment of the classic, for it sets out in precise terms the conception of the project which Voltaire formulated: that is, the desire to fix something which is too changeable, 'volage'. A multiple overdetermination of Racine's wave, then, begins to emerge. The excess which (as La Motte had argued) it represents, is claimed for a classicism whose project entails twice stopping the motion which it figures: firstly, the to-and-fro of the critical discussion of the wave is denied by d'Olivet's repeated assertions of critical homogeneity; and secondly, the wave as a figure, its quality of being 'épouvanté', is claimed by d'Olivet for fixity, as a historical constant of poetic language.

But d'Olivet is not yet finished with Théramène. He next constructs a conversation between 'Théramène, qui vivoit dans les temps héroïques de la Grèce, avec M. de la Motte, vivant au dix-huitiéme siécle de l'Ere Chrétienne' (37). D'Olivet's Théramène claims that 'je raconte ce que j'ai vû, & comme je l'ai vû', and expresses astonishment that La Motte could be ignorant of the fact that 'il n'y a rien sur la terre, ni dans l'eau, ni dans l'aïr, point de fleuve, point de fontaine, point d'arbre, point de plante, qui n'ait une ame' (37). This continuation of the historicist argument, however, leads rapidly to a sleight-of-hand on d'Olivet's part. The problem of the wave, which is properly one of language and poetic figure, is assimilated to the issue of the fabulous in general. 'Mais ce qui m'étonne,' Théramène says, 'c'est qu'un flot *épouvanté* ait pû scandalizer dans une Scene où il s'agit d'un Monstre envoyé par Neptune, & dans une Tragédie dont l'Héroïne est petite-fille du Soleil' (38). It is not language which should be chosen as the battleground of this argument, he continues, for language has the same status as do other productions of the imagination, such as Neptune and the monster: 'En vérité, ce n'étoit pas trop bien prendre son champ de bataille pour attaquer le langage de la Poësie. Quand on aura obtenu de mon imagination qu'elle laisse passer Neptune, & ce Monstre qu'il envoye; rien n'empêche qu'on ne donne du sentiment à un flot' (38). What had begun as a battle over language is transformed into a question of the historical imaginary. The answer to the question which had occupied La Motte and Boileau, the question of how this poetic language relates to the tragedy in which it is pronounced—Is it excessive or not?—is taken for granted. There is no qualitative difference between Racine's language and the inherited details of the tragic action. Language and plot are adequate one to another, and both are products of the imaginary of a distant antiquity.

Pleased with himself, d'Olivet sent two copies of his *Remarques* to Bouhier on 20 March 1738. But by mid-summer (6 July 1738) d'Olivet was complaining to Bouhier that 'à peine mes *Remarques sur Racine* ont-elles paru qu'il a renouvelé ses actes d'hostilité' (ii. 283). The reference is to the abbé Pierre-François Desfontaines (1685–1745) and to his *Racine vengé ou Examen des Remarques grammaticales de M. l'abbé d'Olivet*, which appeared in print only in 1739, but was in circulation the year before.[32] While having to contend with Desfontaines, d'Olivet found himself under attack from another quarter in the *Observations critiques à l'occasion des Remarques de grammaire sur Racine, de monsieur l'abbé d'Olivet, de l'Académie francoise*, printed by Prault in Paris in 1738, and written by Jean Soubeiran de Scopon (1699–1751).[33]

Neither of d'Olivet's interlocutors was opposed to the establishment of the French classic. But Desfontaines did object to d'Olivet's redirection of Boileau's project. As he correctly observed, 'ce qui ne seroit jamais venu, ce me semble, à l'esprit de M. Despreaux, c'est d'exécuter ce projet sur des ouvrages de Poësie' (1). Both Desfontaines and Soubeiran de Scopon sensed that more was at stake in d'Olivet's gesture than simple codification. Soubeiran de Scopon pointed out that d'Olivet's criticism of Racine was not really about Racine, but rather about the impossibility of criticizing Racine, and about the superiority of poetry over prose. 'M. l'Abbé d'Olivet n'a entrepris de critiquer Racine, que pour faire croire qu'on ne pouvait guére le critiquer avec succès' (5–6). Desfontaines, while agreeing with Boileau's idea that 'la France, ainsi que l'Italie, pût avoir ses Auteurs classiques' (1), takes on the historicist project formulated by d'Olivet, but in different terms. The passage of time is not what validates poetic language, but rather what undermines it. Language, he declares, is not fixed and is furthermore not fixable (1–2). In just the space of the fifty or sixty years required, according to d'Olivet, for the establishment of the classic (*Remarques*, 5), the general non-fixity of language, says Desfontaines, can have the opposite effect upon a work: once declared faultless, it can become outdated (2). Further, there is the problem of authority. Even Homer, he argues, cannot be valorized by the simple passage of time, even if it is a great deal of time. 'L'estime, l'admiration même d'un grand nombre de siècles peu éclairez ne prouve rien' (119).

Desfontaines, constructing a 'Dialogue de Theramène qui vivoit dans les tems héroiques, avec M. l'Abbé d'Olivet', has Théramène claim that he has never heard of Moschus the Phoenician, and, further, accuse d'Olivet of turning him, Théramène the sophisticated courtier, into a pedant (107–8). As for the wave, Desfontaines refuses to assimilate the problem which it poses to the artifactual. It remains for him a problem of poetic language, and he analyses the passage of the *récit* in which it occurs as a 'hypotipose', the rhetorical figure which sets the thing before the eyes (89).[34] In this, Desfontaines proved himself a reader of the language philosopher and grammarian Dumarsais, whose *Des tropes* had appeared in 1730.[35] The twelve lines of Racine's *récit* which narrate the appearance of the monster (1513–24) are there used to exemplify the figure of the hypotyposis (134). But Dumarsais goes on to criticize the wave in much the same terms as had La Motte, calling it an inappropriate intrusion from another genre: 'Les figures qui plaisent dans un épithalame, déplaisent dans une oraison funèbre: la tristesse doit parler simplement, si elle veut intéresser' (134).

Accordingly, after repeating Dumarsais on the subject of the hypotyposis, Desfontaines must ignore him on the subject of the wave if he is to avenge Racine, as his title promises. He supplies examples intended to normalize the moment of the wave, and to argue that this moment is not excessive. His examples are not, as were d'Olivet's, instances of other fabulous events in *Phèdre*. Rather, they come from other texts which use the same rhetorical figure. In this series, the logic of example works to retain the theme of bodies of water, while varying the genre from which the examples are drawn. The first two fall roughly within the period of time which is at issue, the preceding fifty or sixty years. He first quotes, from epic poetry, the lines from Voltaire's *Henriade*: 'Et des fleuves français les eaux ensanglantées/ Ne portaient que des morts aux mers épouvantées' (100).[36] His second example of horrified water is drawn from the genre which Dumarsais had argued was the most inappropriate to the figure, that is, the *oraison funèbre*. From the prose oratory of the pulpit Desfontaines cites 'l'océan étonné' from Bossuet's *Oraison funèbre de la Reine d'Angleterre*.[37] Finally, in a move which shatters his time frame, Desfontaines cites, from book 8 of the *Aeneid*: 'Dissultant ripae, refluitque exterritus amnis' (240), 'The river-banks leapt apart, and even the river flowed backwards in alarm.'[38]

In his invocation of Virgil, Desfontaines shows himself to be Boileau's reader; for it is just this line which, in a little-remarked footnote, is the last word of the eleventh *Réflexion critique*.[39] Desfontaines's remark is deceptively flat: 'On peut croire que Racine avait le vers de Virgile dans son esprit, lorsqu'il a fait le sien, & qu'il l'a voulu imiter' (112). But if Desfontaines is indeed reading Boileau at this point, 'to imitate' is nevertheless not a word which occurs in the eleventh *Réflexion critique*. Rather, Boileau constructs there a complex analogical architecture which allows him to surround the figure of the wave, re-integrate it, and re-claim it for a certain kind of homogeneity. Boileau indeed created the possibility for the classic Racine. But his project in doing so had nothing explicitly to do with the classic or its establishment which, as we recall, he thought should be based on prose translations. Rather, Boileau wanted to be able to call the wave sublime. He showed that the wave belongs to a certain critical structure, and it is just this structuring which d'Olivet and

Desfontaines took up twenty-five years later in order to produce the classic.

In the eleventh *Réflexion critique*, Boileau does not shy away from the substance of La Motte's critique of the wave. That critique had aimed at the voice of the poet, and the genres in which it can make itself heard appropriately. Possessed by poetic fury, the poet's voice can be heard in the ode, La Motte had argued, but not in a genre such as tragedy, in which only the voice of the characters must be heard. The personification of inanimate objects may be heard (or so La Motte's argument, as paraphrased by Boileau in the eleventh *Réflexion critique*, would go) 'quand c'est le Poëte qui parle, parce qu'il est supposé espris de fureur; mais [...] il n'en est pas de mesme des Personnages qu'on fait parler' (182). Boileau's response is simple: 'J'avouë que ces Personnages ne sont pas d'ordinaire supposez espris de fureur; mais ils peuvent l'estre d'une autre passion, et telle qu'est celle de Theramene, qui ne leur fera pas dire des choses moins fortes et moins exaggerées que celles que pourroit dire un Poëte en fureur' (182). Boileau illustrates his point by another monumental moment of story-telling: the recounting by Aeneas, in the second book of the *Aeneid*, of the fall of Troy. 'Ainsi', he begins, 'Enée, dans l'accablement de douleur où il est au commencement du second Livre de l'Eneide, lors qu'il raconte la miserable fin de sa patrie, ne cede pas en audace d'expression à Virgile mesme' (182). The comparison which Boileau is constructing touches three points: those of the two voices, that of Aeneas and that of Virgil, and that of the situation, the telling of a miserable end from within overwhelming sorrow. The very strength of the analogy has already served to deflect the discussion from the obvious La Mottian objection to this example: these issues are genre-specific, and the Virgilian epic cannot correspond to the Racinian tragedy. Like a dream within a dream, Boileau proceeds to place an analogical moment within the general analogy.

> se comparant à un grand arbre, que les Laboureurs s'efforcent d'abbatre à coups de coignée, il [Aeneas] ne se contente pas de prester de la colere à cet arbre, mais luy fait faire des menaces à ces Laboureurs. 'L'arbre indigné, dit-il, les menace en branlant sa teste cheveluë':
>
> Illa usque minatur,
> Et tremefacta comam concusso vertice nutat. (182–3)

Boileau has produced a major shift in the Virgilian text. Call it a misreading—but even a passing acquaintance with Boileau the critic would lead one to suspect that it is deliberately and cunningly undertaken.

La Motte himself took issue with this example, as did Boileau's subsequent editors. First, says La Motte in his 1713 'Réponse à M. Despréaux',[40] the line in question is found towards the end of the second book, not at its beginning. Secondly and more importantly, Boileau's reading is both generally and specifically incorrect, because the comparison of the passage is not between the speaking voice, Aeneas, and the tree, but rather between Troy in flames and the tree; and the lines specifically cited do not imply sentiment attributed to the tree, but 'ne signifient que l'ébranlement et les secousses violentes de l'arbre sous la cognée des laboureurs' (119). Posterity has agreed with La Motte. His 1859 editor noted, 'Ces remarques sont exactes' (119, note 1), and the Belles Lettres edition of Boileau's *Réflexions critiques* reports that 'Boileau s'est trompé' (317, note 23), and refers to 'l'erreur de Boileau', his 'contre-sens' (318, note 24).

But those whose task has been to engage the fact of Boileau's example have perhaps neglected the sweep of his critical project. The tree comparison occurs at the moment in Aeneas' narration when he recalls himself standing upon the rooftop, watching Neptune's destruction of that city which is proper to him: 'There, Neptune himself is at work shattering the walls and the foundations dislodged by his mighty trident, and tearing the whole city from its site' (69).[41] And it is in fact—this point must be granted to La Motte and his readers—to the city of Troy, and not to Aeneas himself, that the voice of Aeneas compares the tree hacked by iron: 'And in truth all Illium was now, visibly before me, settling into the fires, and Neptune's own Troy, uprooted, was overturning; like an ancient rowan-tree' (69).[42] The central image, the great tree which is struck, is analogous not to the one who tells the story, but rather to what the story is telling, its object. Troy can be uprooted ('ex imo', 625) just as the tree can be felled: 'till gradually vanquished it gives a final groan, and at last overcome by the wounds and wrenched from its place it trails havoc down the mountainside' (69).[43] These are two monumental images of something coming loose from its foundations, being torn out of its rootedness, being free to circulate and falling down, and leaving ruin in its wake.

However, there is a kind of truth in Boileau's claim that Aeneas compares himself to the great tree. For the passage continues, 'I climbed down from the roof, and with the goddess guiding me won my way between the flames and the foes. The weapons let me through; the fires drew back from me' (69).[44] This is a third image of descent and circulation, and with this third superpositioning, the lines of the analogy become suitably confused. Théramène is, like Aeneas, the teller of Neptune's act of destruction. Hippolyte and Troy, both of whose miserable ends are being recounted, then become coincident, and the voice of Aeneas equals the voice of Théramène. But the teller of the story, the one who is stricken and falls like his own city, like the tree, is also the one from whom an elemental force draws back. The wave of Racine runs back, and the flames of Virgil draw back ('recedunt', 633). Aeneas is coincident not with Théramène but rather with the monster. The teller and the object of the telling are confounded.

Accordingly, however true it may be that Boileau got the crude lines of his reading wrong, nevertheless, even in being wrong he is right. In fastening upon the text's hyperbole, Boileau succeeds in making the only point which interests him. Both this passage, and, by analogy, Racine's, are sublime. Circulation, confounding and confusion of agent and client are signs that one is in the presence of the sublime. At the beginning of the twelfth *Réflexion critique*, Boileau quotes the description of this effect from Chapter V of Longinus: 'Car tout ce qui est veritablement sublime a cela de propre, quand on l'escoute, qu'il esleve l'ame, et luy fait concevoir une plus haute opinion d'elle-mesme, la remplissant de joye, et de je ne sçay quel noble orgueil, comme si c'estoit elle qui eust produit les choses qu'elle vient simplement d'entendre' (184). This description of the sublime requires a confusion of speaker and listener. In the presence of the sublime, the important factor is not the origination, but the sublimity of the figure itself. Paradoxically, that sublimity can be known precisely by means of confusion, by the confusion of agency which it produces. In scenes of telling, the teller both obviously is, but perhaps more interestingly and importantly is also not, the point. The sublime has action: it cuts loose, is torn up from its foundations, like Troy, the tree and Aeneas. It most importantly is not rooted. Thus, the critique of the voice in the discussion of the wave is countered.

Lest there be any doubt that Boileau intends the lines of his grand analogy to be extended, the verb for the striking action of the sublime, 'frapper', is insisted upon in the passage which immediately follows the example from Virgil: 'Lors qu'un endroit d'un Discours frappe tout le monde, il ne faut pas chercher des raisons, ou plustost de vaines subtilitez, pour s'empescher d'en estre frappé; mais faire si bien que nous trouvions nous-mesmes les raisons pour-quoy il nous frappe' (183). This thrice-repeated striking is exactly what the farmers have just been doing to the tree. The extended lines of the analogy thus secure Boileau's point: whereas it had seemed as though the sublime example were the tree, it is at the same time the much-ignored farmers who do what the sublime does. A location impossible to locate; confusion of agency; and, not incidentally, another case of Boileau's own text performing exactly what it advocates.

By means of this complex argument-by-exemplarity, Boileau argues for the sublimity of the voice of Théramène. The Virgilian analogy to the wave must be understood in the context of this argument. The reference is to another scene of telling which is also a scene of uprooting: the eighth book, in which King Evander recounts to Aeneas how Hercules saved his people from Cacus, 'a man-monster of hideous aspect' (206) who lives in a deep cave on a mountain:

> Now there was a pinnacle of flint-rock which stood sheer, as if the stone had been cut away all round it, soaring to a dizzy height on the ridge above the cave; an impressive sight and a fit nesting-place for sinister birds of prey. It was inclined towards the downward slope, leaning towards the river on the left. Hercules now strained at it from the right side, pressing it forwards. He shook it, wrenched it from its roots, and then gave it a sudden thrust. At that thrust the great sky thundered, the river-banks leapt apart, and even the river flowed backwards in alarm. (208)[45]

There is something distinctly tree-like about this crag-rock: birds nest in it; it stands high on a mountainside; and it has, precisely, roots. Once again, it is the pulling up of something from its roots (*radicibus*, 238) which precedes and produces the textual moment of the hyperbole, the alarm of the river and its flowing backwards.

This is the homogenization-work by means of which Boileau recuperates the wave of the *récit de Théramène*. The point is to show that the figure of the wave is sublime, that it is adequate to a sublime moment, the arrival of the monster, and that the problem of poetic voice is not only not nearly as simple as La Motte would have it be, but also undetermining in this kind of question precisely because it is undeterminable. If the voice of the poet is sublime, then it is by definition unlocatable, forever rootless and circulating.

It is difficult to resist the conclusion that Boileau is engaged in a meta-level pun on the proper name of Racine: the tree severed from its roots, Troy torn up from its foundations by Neptune, the rocky crag uprooted by Hercules. It is not the *racine* which is sublime, the argument would accordingly go, but rather that which is produced from and identifiable by the lack of *racine*, and, at the same time, the lack of Racine, the unlocatability, that is, of the tragic voice in the poet himself. The voice of the poet disappears utterly into the text, and there is no longer Racine. In the wake of this argument, however, there is a 'Racine', a text whose excessiveness has been smoothed out and claimed for the sublime. It is thus an inheritable text.

If one consults the *Oxford English Dictionary* entry, 'classic', one finds that an early reference to its use in the sense of 'in the style of the literature and art of Greek and Latin antiquity' is in 1744, by William Collins, in the *Epistle to Thomas Hanmer*, and that the reference is to Racine: 'And classic Judgement gain'd to sweet Racine/ The temp'rate strength of Maro's chaster line' (73–4).[46] The classic in the English language too is defined by the double reference to Racine and to Virgil. This choice of the texts by which to name the classic accords, as we have seen, with the French formulation. The project of classicism was to stand as a bulwark against change and decline in language and taste. The classic is a limit, a notion of a borderline. Surely, if this operation depends precisely upon motion and circulation, upon the lack of fixity and locatability of the voice, then the situation is historically ironic. The problematic of the wave of the *récit de Théramène* has revealed that, in the inheritance of the text of Racine a quarter-century later, there has been not just a loss of Boileau's critical terms and structure, but, far more radically, a precise reversal. At the level of Racine's language, the excess Boileau had recuperated by the critical act of setting it in motion is claimed for an eternalized fixity. Boileau's anti-*racine* policy has been reversed and turned into 'Racine'.

The twelfth and final *Réflexion critique* stands apart as the only one of the series which does not have a specific target. Its main occasion is Boileau's sense that he must supply 'au defaut de Longin' a definition of the sublime. This he does. It is a three-part definition, and, says Boileau, if one wants examples of each of the three qualities of the sublime, either the treatise of Longinus itself, or Boileau's own tenth *Réflexion critique*, which is an extended discussion of Longinus' example from *Genesis*, as well as the examples of the sublime which first appeared in Boileau's 1701 Preface, may be consulted. It seems a logical extension of the project which occupied the 1701 Preface: in the wake of his thoroughgoing re-exemplification of the sublime, his making the sublime French both linguistically and allegorically by force of example, Boileau now moves into a Longinian lacuna, supplies a definition of the sublime, and thus becomes a kind of hyper-Longinus, a Longinus-plus-Boileau, who has filled an absence. But this is not just any absence; it is the filling of a precisely definitive absence. Boileau's final move is to become the new Longinus.

The problem of the example, however, remains. Boileau deems it necessary to supply a master example, in which all three of the qualities of the sublime are united. The example given by the new Longinus of the newly defined sublime comes from the Racine of *Athalie*. Since ancient sites are being re-occupied—the place of Longinus taken by Boileau, the place of the sublime taken by the new definition—we might ask at this point: into the place of what does the new example move?

While the example from the treatise of Longinus which is the most historically astonishing is from Genesis, the much-commented *fiat lux*, Longinus introduces this example with an 'Ainsi'. The example which immediately precedes it is from the *Iliad*. Both are found in the chapter of the treatise which is the seventh in Boileau's translation, but has generally been handed down as the ninth. Its subject is the relationship between the poet or orator and his poem or oration, and its argument is that, at its best, there is a correspondence and an adequacy between the *esprit* of the speaker and the sublimity of his words. In order to speak as Alexander, here in his reply to Parmenion, it is necessary to be Alexander: 'N'est-il pas vrai qu'il falloit estre Alexandre pour faire cette réponse?' (62).[47] The Homer of the *Iliad* is himself heroic when he writes of heroes, and, if the *Iliad* is full of ardour and force, it is because Homer composed it 'durant que son esprit estoit en sa plus grande vigueur' (66).

The example given to illustrate this situation, and the one which immediately elicits the 'Ainsi' of the Biblical example, is from the epiphany of Poseidon, the beginning of Book 13 of the *Iliad*. Poseidon descends from the mountaintop on the island of Samothrace and drives his chariot over the waves to reach the Achaians, who are much in need, at this point, of his encouragement:

Neptune ainsi marchant dans ces vastes campagnes
Fait trembler sous ses piés et forests et montagnes.
[...]
Il attelle son char, et montant fierement
Lui fait fendre les flots de l'humide Element.
Dés qu'on le voit marcher sur ces liquides plaines
D'aise on entend sauter les pezantes Balaînes.
L'Eau fremit sous le Dieu qui lui donne la loi,
Et semble avec plaisir reconnoistre son Roi.
Cependant le char vole, etc. (64)

This is, according to Longinus, Homer at his best: neither inappropriately mixing up human predicaments with the divine, nor yet fallen into the decline of the *Odyssey*, the poet is precisely adequate to his subject. But there is a problem with this, the height of Homer and the central example of Longinus. Boileau has rearranged one of the sides of the equation, the text.

It would be a mistake to expect literal accuracy from Boileau's translating effort.[48] In the preface to his edition, he is clear about the liberty which he has taken:

Qu'on ne s'attende pas pourtant de trouver ici une version timide et scrupuleuse des paroles de Longin. Bien que je me sois efforcé de ne me point écarter en pas un endroit des regles de la veritable traduction; je me suis pourtant donné une honneste liberté, sur tout dans les passages qu'il rapporte. J'ai songé qu'il ne s'agissoit pas simplement ici de traduire Longin; mais de donner au Public un Traité du Sublime qui pût estre utile. (44)

Boileau was apt simply to omit from Longinus those passages which were too Greek or corrupt, to fill in manuscript lacunae with transitions of his own and to gloss and replace the rhetorical vocabulary of the treatise with less technical expressions. This is, moreover, an attitude towards translation which had a seventeenth-century history in the 'belles infidèles' of d'Ablancourt, and which would have a future in the 'querelle d'Homère'.[49] But, while Boileau's translating ethos has been, with respect to these kinds of changes, frequently indicated and contextualized, it has perhaps not been noticed that, in the following case, the changes which he introduced into the treatise can be attributed to a much more precise motivation than that of public utility.

The second and third editions of Boileau's translation appeared in 1683 and 1685, and, for the 1683 edition, he expanded the series of translator's remarks which he had included in the original, 1674, edition in order to take account of the criticisms of André Dacier. Dacier's comment on Boileau's translation of Neptune's march reads as follows:

> *Dés qu'on le voit marcher sur ces liquides plaines.*—Ces vers sont fort nobles et fort beaux; mais ils n'expriment pas la pensée d'Homere, qui dit que lorsque Neptune commence à marcher, les Baleines sautent de tous costez devant lui et reconnoissent leur Roi; que de joie, la mer se fend pour lui faire place. Monsieur D*** dit de l'eau ce qu'Homere dit des Baleines, et il s'est contenté d'exprimer un petit fremissement qui arrive sous les moindres barques comme sous les plus grands vaisseaux au lieu de nous representer aprés Homere des flots entr'ouverts et une mer qui se separe. (240, note 18)

Dacier's objection goes to two points: firstly, Boileau has transferred the recognition-factor from the whales to the water; and secondly, Boileau has minimized the effect. 'L'Eau fremit', according to Boileau, but, according to Homer, 'the sea stood apart before him', as one recent translation has it.[50]

But there is another issue which does not come out as clearly in Dacier's criticism. Where Dacier has Homer say that 'de joie, la mer se fend pour lui faire place', and, for purposes of comparison, a recent English translation has 'the sea stood apart before him, rejoicing' (272), Boileau has translated, 'L'Eau semble avec plaisir reconnoistre son Roi'. Boileau has subtracted from Homer the attribution of passion to the sea; both the sea's rejoicing and its recognition of its governing deity are reduced to a semblance.

Things become yet more complicated with Boileau's reply to Dacier's criticism, in which is hidden a manifesto of the poetics of translation which goes far beyond what Boileau's preface had called his 'honneste liberté':

> *Fremit sous le Dieu qui luy donne la loi.*—Il y a dans le Grec, que l'eau en voyant Neptune, se ridoit, et *sembloit soûrire de joye.* Mais cela seroit trop dur en nostre langue. Au reste, j'ai crû que *l'eau reconnoist son Roy*, seroit quelque chose de plus sublime que de mettre, comme il y a dans le Grec, que *les Baleines reconnoissent leur Roy.* J'ay tâché dans les passages qui sont rapportez d'Homere, à encherir sur lui, plûtost que de le suivre trop scrupuleusement à la piste. (200)

This is not a counter-argument. Rather, it is the effect of a radically different notion of the project of translation from that which a Dacier would advocate. That different notion is covered by Boileau's attempt to 'encherir sur' Homer, rather than scrupulously following his trail. The metaphor of the following of a path was, along with apian, digestive, filian, echoic and choral metaphors, a standard *topos* for the imitation of the ancients, and had been since the Renaissance.[51] Boileau, the fierce partisan of the ancients, abandons it in favour of something called 'encherir sur'. In this translator's note, he reveals himself to be not the faithful defender of the ancients, but rather the most modern of the moderns: Homer, at what Longinus claims is his most sublime, his most consonant with his own text, can be improved upon, and has been. That is Boileau's defence.

Two things are important about this tangled translation problem: first, Boileau has written out of the Homeric text the very problem which will prompt such a virtuosic performance on his part in the eleventh *Réflexion critique*: the problem of the text's attribution of passion to the sea. Dacier's criticism appeared only in the 1683 and 1685 editions of Boileau's translation. At the moment when he prefaced his 1701 edition of his *Œuvres complètes* with the important series of re-exemplifications which included for the first time his unappreciative remarks on the sword of Théophile's *Pyrame et Thisbée*, the text of Dacier's critique of this translation of Homer disappeared from his edition. His own remark remained, but it appeared as assertion, apparently in response to nothing. Any mention of Homer's attribution of passion to the sea was gone.

What this means, secondly, is that, if Homer, and especially the Homer of the *Iliad*, may be said to be the master example in Longinus that even the Biblical example is 'like', then that example is not precisely the Homer of the *Iliad*. That Homer is already gone from Boileau's translation. Into that place has moved a new Homer, explicitly improved and made 'more sublime' by Boileau.

How may one re-exemplify something which one had always been in the process of re-exemplifying in the first place? This is the problem with the answer to the question: Into what place does the example from Racine move in Boileau's twelfth *Réflexion critique*? It is easy enough to see that, as the one example given, it moves into the place of Homer. But what was that place, in the first place? There never was, it seems, any first place. Homer never occupied Homer's place, unless translated by Boileau, and made more sublime than Homer. The example from Racine's *Athalie* occupies a place–no-place; the old place of the exemplary had always been the no-place of something completely new. Racine becomes the new Homer, but there was never any old Homer. The example itself plays on this problem in a cunning and remarkable way.

The quotation is from the first scene of *Athalie*, and Abner has just expressed to the high priest, Joad, his fear that the fury of Athalie will cause her to attack God in his very temple:

A quoy ce Grand Prestre, sans s'esmouvoir, respond:

> Celuy qui met un frein à la fureur des flots,
> Sçait aussi des meschants arrester les complots.
> Soumis avec respect à sa volonté sainte,
> Je crains Dieu, cher Abner, et n'ay point d'autre crainte. (185)

The speaking voice, 'sans s'émouvoir', represents a sea without motion, and puts a brake on the fury of the waves. The force of the sublime example is the arresting of all motion, and of all passion, both in the speaker and in the text. The connection is clear: this example connects itself thematically with the wave of the *récit de Théramène*. Just as in Longinus a certain thematic, that of light, for one, may be seen to connect his examples in ways which have nothing obvious to do with the rhetorical point under discussion,[52] so in Boileau the wave of *Athalie* dialogues with the wave which was the subject of the previous *Réflexion*. The wave which had been horrified by the monster is here stilled. The brakes are put on it and its hyperbole. Fear remains in the passage, 'Je crains Dieu', but it is the fear of the paradoxical expression, 'god-fearing', the fear productive of sobriety, calm and quiet. This fear of God is equivalent to confidence in God, as Boileau will conclude with Joad's 'parfaite confiance en Dieu'. It is a fear located not in an animated inanimate nature, but rather in man, the high priest Joad. The final word of Boileau's *Réflexion* is 'Israëlite', and, through a spectacular series of transmutations, he has transformed the horror of the wave at the monster into the fear of God of the high priest. Joad becomes an anti-Théramène.

It should by this point be apparent that the structure which we noticed operating on the establishment by d'Olivet of the classic Racine, that is, the yearning for a return and the consequent loss of the object which was never fully known in the first place, governs as well the position of Homer into which Boileau transposes Racine. In effect, there is no Homer, but only 'Homer'. I have claimed that this is the structure of nostalgia.

The term 'nostalgia' is from the Greek *nostos*, 'return home', and *algos*, 'pain', or, as the eleventh edition of the *Encyclopedia Britannica* translates it, in a locution which brings out the work of mourning involved, 'grief'. The word is unknown to Furetière and the writers of the *Encyclopédie*, but it comes into English in the eighteenth century. According to the *OED*, it was a medical term for a disease identified by physicians as severe homesickness. The context of one early attestation is a voyage of discovery, from the journal of James Cook.

From an anchorage off the coast of New Guinea on Monday, 3 September 1770, the captain went ashore with a small group of men. It was an impatient gesture, for he was already determined to leave:

> I went a shore in the Pinnace accompanied by Mr Banks and Dr Solander, having a mind to land once in this Country before we quit it altogether which I now am determined to do without delay; for I found that it is only spending time to little purpose and carrying us far out of our way staying upon this coast, which is so shallow that we can hardly keep within sight of land.[53]

The landing party was attacked by the inhabitants and, outnumbered, beat a hasty retreat. Upon returning to the ship, Cook made good upon his determination to leave, and an interlinear hand reports that it was

> to the No small satisfaction of I beleive three fourths of our company, the sick became well & the melancholy lookd gay. The greatest part of them were now pretty far gone with the longing for home which the Physicians have gone so far as to esteem a disease under the name of Nostalgia; indeed I can find hardly any body in the ship clear of its effects but the Captn Dr Solander & myself, indeed we three have pretty constant employment for our minds which I beleive to be the best if not the only remedy for it. (409, note 4)

This is a counter-intuitive prescription: one remedy for nostalgia may be setting sail, but 'the best if not the only remedy for it' is not that. This perhaps implies that home is not the most effective remedy for nostalgia because there is no home, but only 'home'. Nostalgia declares itself among sailors subject to current anxieties such as attacks upon them by the inhabitants of the coast, and they then mobilize what is both past and distant, 'home', in order to give direction to the departure from that anxiety.

If it is correct that the project of the classic fits into the general structure of nostalgia, then 'Racine' is 'home'. The Racinian text is an image of rootedness mobilized from within a current set of anxieties which includes an overwhelming sense of loss, decline and attack, from Boileau's evocation of an Athalie apt to *attaquer Dieu*, to d'Olivet's sense of being under attack from café society. The irony of the structure is that the home to which the return is effected is not a place but rather a construction which depends upon a forgetting of its object. 'Homer', and consequently 'Racine', were never integral as sites, but were always fractured by the work of mourning. *Trauer* produces canons and classics, and, if *Phèdre* emerges at the other end of the eighteenth century as a 'Trauerspiel' in Friedrich Schiller's 1804 translation,[54] then the reading-work which constructed 'Racine' is a play of mourning on a play of mourning.

And is this not the activity which engages Théramène in the famous *récit*? If readers of Racine from then to now have been drawn to his lengthy threnody, that to which they are drawn may indeed be said to be a scene of mourning and the language of grief. This is the high Racinian moment of *algos*, the telling of the loss of a Prince to the father who killed him. We the readers supply the *nostos*, and the *récit de Théramène* becomes a mirror of the process which constructed 'Racine'. To tell of loss and speak with passion, and yet to be activated precisely by a forgetting and misrecognition of the 'triste objet' which has been fractured, torn asunder: Théramène's report depends upon a triple gulf. First the horses: 'Ils ne connaissent plus ni le frein ni la voix' (1536); and then the fantasized eye of the father: 'Et que méconnaîtrait l'oeil même de son père' (1570); and then Aricie: 'Et ne connaissant plus ce héros qu'elle adore' (1581).

This memory which is activated by and depends upon forgetting can precisely be called history. Indeed, Leo Spitzer once read Théramène as a historian, not just as 'the appointed historian of Thésée's family', but also as 'a humanistic historiographer who can teach only in a lengthy and ornate fashion, because history is a solemn and sad spectacle'.[55] It has more recently been claimed that a history which has promoted memory as its centre is a spectacular act of mourning, the lost object which promotes this memorial history being nothing other than literature itself.[56] And yet, the logic of 'Racine' suggests that that literature was only ever a *Trauerspiel*, and that the very act of reading it in the 'first' place had originarily what Peter France has formulated as the status of being 'too late'.[57] If this logic holds, then *Phèdre* both sets up the structure within which literature can be instituted, and figures the impossibility of that institution. It both thematically plays out the situational particularity of being too late, and, in coming to it, its readers have always been tardy. Out of this structure *en abîme*, we may now be unsurprised that Théramène's *récit* is characterized by 'une hyper-véracité artificielle du passé'.[58] For Spitzer's sad and solemn spectacle is understood differently now. And the mourning which writes of its passing clings for dear life to artifice.

Postscript: The Wave

In all probability, Racine never saw the sea. One source which enables this statement to be made with relative certainty is the *Mémoire* of Racine's son Louis, which Raymond Picard called 'la Légende Dorée de Jean Racine'.[59] We owe the existence of this memoir to the grandson, also named Jean Racine, of the Racine who had never seen the sea, for Louis set it down for him, that he might know the truth about his grandfather. This Jean Racine, grandson, was, as it happened, killed by a wave: the tidal wave produced at Cadiz by the Lisbon earthquake of 1755.[60]

Notes to chapter 4

1. Adrien Thomas Perdou de Subligny, *Dissertation sur les tragédies de Phèdre et d'Hippolyte* (Paris: Sercy, 1677), 53–4.
2. Peter France, 'Hyperbole', in *Politeness and its Discontents. Problems in French Classical Culture* (Cambridge: Cambridge University Press, 1992), 11–26.
3. See the introduction to Pradon's *Phèdre et Hippolyte*, ed. O. Classe (Exeter: University of Exeter, 1987), pp. xii-xxii.
4. Antoine Houdart de La Motte, *Les Paradoxes littéraires ou discours écrits par cet académicien*, ed. B. Julien (1859; Geneva: Slatkine, 1971), 111.
5. *Les Paradoxes*, 78–110, reproduces the 1713 edition. It had gone through a second edition in 1709.
6. Paul Mesnard (ed.), *Œuvres de J. Racine* (Paris: Hachette, 1865), iii. 275.
7. In Nicolas Boileau-Despréaux, *Dialogues, Réflexions critiques, Œuvres diverses*, ed. Charles-H. Boudhors (Paris: Belles Lettres, 1960).
8. 'Réponse à la onzième Réflexion de Monsieur Despréaux sur Longin', in *Les Paradoxes littéraires*, 111–20.
9. François de Salignac de La Mothe-Fénelon, *Lettre à l'Académie* (Paris: Droz, 1970), 93.
10. Louis Racine, *Œuvres complètes* (1808; Geneva: Slatkine, 1969).
11. Theodore Besterman (ed.), *Voltaire's Correspondance* (Geneva: Institut et musée Voltaire, 1959), xlv. 274.
12. Claude Favre de Vaugelas, *Remarques sur la langue françoise*, ed. Jeanne Streicher (Paris: Droz, 1934), Preface, unnumbered pages.

13. Quoted in Timothy Murray, 'The Académie Française', in *A New History of French Literature*, ed. Denis Hollier (Cambridge and London: Harvard University Press, 1989), 267–73 (272).
14. Michael Moriarty, *Taste and Ideology in Seventeenth-Century France* (Cambridge: Cambridge University Press, 1988).
15. *Voltaire's Correspondence*, xlv. 275.
16. For d'Olivet's biography, see the *Correspondance littéraire du president Bouhier, No. 3, lettres de Pierre-Joseph Thoulier abbé d'Olivet (1719–1745)* (Université de Saint-Etienne, 1976), i. 3–10.
17. Letter of 27 Sept. 1737; *Correspondance*, ii. 257.
18. *Correspondance*, i. 9.
19. See Lucien Brunel, *Les Philosophes et l'Académie française au dix-huitième siècle* (Paris: Hachette, 1884), 1–27.
20. Paul Mesnard, *Histoire de l'Académie française depuis sa fondation jusqu'en 1830* (Paris: Charpentier, 1857), 94.
21. D'Olivet writes to Bouhier on 15 Sept. 1730 that he is about to depart for Holland and mentions, in his next letter, dated 4 Nov. 1730, 'les cinquante jours que j'ai été hors de Paris' (151). On 10 Jan. 1731 he writes that 'j'étais gai comme un pinson je jour que je rentrai dans Paris, à mon retour de Hollande. Mais dès le lendemain je perdis la tête; et pendant deux mois, ou peu s'en faut, j'ai été le plus à plaindre de tous les hommes puisque j'étais le moins raisonnable' (157).
22. Letter of 4 Feb. 1731; *Correspondance*, i. 159. D'Olivet affects the third person in relating the story to Bouhier. The comment of his editors is: 'Il ne fait aucun doute que d'Olivet raconte là sa propre histoire' (i. 160 n. 1).
23. François Ravaisson, *Archives de la Bastille* (Paris: A. Durand et Pedone-Lauriel, 1867), xii. 150.
24. Letter of 22 Dec. 1737; *Correspondance*, ii. 263.
25. For the status of translation as a genre to about the mid-1660s, see Roger Zuber, *Les 'Belles Infidèles' et la formation du goût classique. Perrot d'Ablancourt et Guez de Balzac* (Paris: Armand Colin, 1968). Zuber is aware of d'Olivet's report, but is sceptical of its accuracy and reads over its nuances as simply 'défavorables aux traducteurs', 140 n. 2.
26. Nicolas Boileau (trans.), *Traité du sublime, ou du merveilleux dans le discours* (Paris: Belles Lettres, 1942), 61–2.
27. Nicolas Boileau, *Satires, Epîtres, Art poétique* (Paris: Gallimard, 1985), 50.
28. There are no chapter headings in the manuscript source. The chapter in question is called in one modern translation, 'False Wit'. Trans. James M. Arieti and John M. Grosset (New York and Toronto: Edwin Mellen Press, 1985).
29. Paul Pellison Fontanier and l'abbé d'Olivet, *Histoire de l'Académie française* (Paris: Didier, 1858), ii. 47. His 19th-cent. editor found d'Olivet's declaration to be incomprehensible: 'Il est étrange que d'Olivet [...] n'ait pas regardé comme classiques les grands auteurs du dix-septième siècle', 47 n. 1. By 1858, clearly, the eternalization of the French classic was so accomplished that the editor then forcibly misreads d'Olivet's simple statement: 'On s'expliquerait tout au plus qu'il dit qu'au temps où fut commencé le dictionnaire, nous n'avions pas d'auteurs reconnus pour classiques.'
30. On the heritage of d'Olivet's appeal to 'toute la France', see Moriarty, *Taste and Ideology*, esp. ch. 7, 'Boileau: taste and the institution of "literature"', 171–88.

31. The connection between Théophile's sword and Racine's wave was however commented upon in a review of the 1713 edition of Boileau's *Œuvres*. *Journal literaire* 2 (Sept.–Oct. 1713), 40–63 (61–2).
32. We learn from d'Olivet's letter of 14 Oct. 1738 that '*Racine vengé*, ouvrage promis par l'abbé Desfontaines, n'a point paru' (ii. 293).
33. 'C'est un Toulousain', d'Olivet reports in the letter of 12 Jan. 1739, 'fils ou frère de conseiller au parlement' (ii. 294).
34. 'A vivid description of a scene, event, or situation, bringing it, as it were, before the eyes of the hearer or reader'. *OED*. For further references, see Ch. 2, n. 2.
35. César Chesneau, sieur du Marsais, *Des tropes ou des différents sens, Figure et vingt autres articles de l'Encyclopédie, suivis de l'Abrégé des tropes de l'abbé Ducros* (Paris: Flammarion, 1988).
36. O. R. Taylor (ed.), *La Henriade*, in *The Complete Works of Voltaire* (Geneva: Institut et musée Voltaire, 1970), ii. 357 (chant II).
37. 'Oraison funèbre de Henriette-Marie de France, Reine de la Grand'Bretagne', *Oraisons funèbres* (Paris: Garnier, 1961), 112: 'L'Océan étonné de se voir traversé tant de fois en des appareils si divers, et pour des causes si différentes'.
38. Virgil, *The Aeneid*, trans. W. F. Jackson Knight (Harmondsworth: Penguin, 1956), 208.
39. Lancaster missed this move on Boileau's part, being under the impression that 'Mesnard showed that the line was inspired by Vergil'. *A History of French Dramatic Literature in the Seventeenth Century*, iv, pt. 1, 109–10 n. 17.
40. *Les Paradoxes littéraires* (1859; Geneva: Slatkine, 1971), 111–20.
41. 'Neptunus muros magnoque emota tridenti/ fundamenta quatit totamque a sedibus urbem/ eruit' (610–12).
42. 'Tum vero omne mihi visum considere in ignis/ Ilium et ex imo verti Neptunia Troia;/ ac veluti summis antiquam in montibus ornum' (624–6).
43. 'Vulneribus donec paulatim evicta supremum/ congemuit traxitque iugis avulsa ruinam' (630–1).
44. 'Descendo ac decente deo flammam inter et hostis/ expedior: dant tela locum flammaeque recedunt' (633–4).
45. 'Stabat acuta silex praecisis undique saxis/ speluncae dorso insurgens, altissima visu/ dirarum nidis domus opportuna volucrum./ hanc, ut prona iugo laeuum incumbebat ad amnem,/ dexter in adversum nitens concussit et imis/ avulsam soluit radicibus, inde repente/ impulsit; impulsu quo maximus intonat aether,/ dissultant ripae refluitque exterritus amnis' (233–40).
46. Richard Wendorf and Charles Ryskamp (eds.), *The Works of William Collins* (Oxford: Clarendon Press, 1979), 18.
47. This sentence belongs to an interpolation supplied by Boileau in response to a 6-leaf manuscript lacuna.
48. Jules Brody has described Boileau's Longinus as 'a calculated act of vulgarization'. *Boileau and Longinus* (Geneva: Droz, 1958), 20.
49. On d'Ablancourt, see Zuber, *Les Belles Infidèles*; for a concise overview of the translation problematic, see R. W. Ladborough, 'Translation from the Ancients in Seventeenth-Century France', *Journal of the Warburg Institute* 2 (1938), 85–104. On the 'querelle d'Homère', see Théodore A. Litman, *Le Sublime en France (1660–1714)* (Paris: Nizet, 1971), 193–5.

50. Richard Lattimore (trans.), *The Iliad of Homer* (Chicago and London: University of Chicago Press, 1951), 272.
51. See G. W. Pigman, III, 'Versions of Imitation in the Renaissance', *Renaissance Quarterly* 33 (1980), 1–23.
52. See Neil Hertz, 'A Reading of Longinus', in *The End of the Line: Essays on Psychoanalysis and the Sublime* (New York: Columbia University Press, 1985), 1–20.
53. J. C. Beaglehole (ed.), *The Voyage of the Endeavour 1768–1771* (Cambridge: Cambridge University Press, 1955), 408.
54. *Phädra. Trauerspiel in fünf Aufzügen* (Stuttgart: Reclam, 1955).
55. Leo Spitzer, 'The "Récit de Théramène"' in *Linguistics and Literary History. Essays in Stylistics* (Princeton: Princeton University Press, 1948), 87–134 (104).
56. Pierre Nora, 'Entre mémoire et histoire. La Problématique des lieux', in *Les Lieux de mémoire* (Paris: Gallimard, 1984), p. xlii.
57. Peter France, 'Myth and Modernity: Racine's *Phèdre*', in *Politeness and its Discontents. Problems in French Classical Culture* (Cambridge: Cambridge University Press, 1992), 40–50.
58. Nora, 'Entre mémoire et histoire', p. xxxiv.
59. Raymond Picard (ed.), *Racine. Œuvres complètes* (Paris: Gallimard, 1950), i. 21.
60. Picard (ed.), *Racine*, i. 1059, n. 1.

WORKS CITED

ADAMS, W. H., *The French Garden 1500–1800* (London: Scholar Press, 1979).

AIMÉ-MARTIN, L. (ed.), *Œuvres complètes de J. Racine avec les notes de tous les commentateurs*, 5th edn. (Paris: Lefèvre et Furne, 1844).

ALPERS, SVETLANA, *The Making of Rubens* (New Haven and London: Yale University Press, 1995).

—— 'Manner and Meaning in Some Rubens Mythologies', *Journal of the Warburg and Courtauld Institutes*, 30 (1967), 272–95.

ANTHONY, JAMES R., *French Baroque Music from Beaujoyeulx to Rameau* (New York: Norton, 1974).

APOSTOLIDÈS, JEAN-MARIE, *Le Roi-machine. Spectacle et politique au temps de Louis XIV* (Paris: Minuit, 1981).

ARIETI, JAMES M., and GROSSET, JOHN M., *Longinus. On the Sublime* (New York and Toronto: Edwin Mellen Press, 1985).

ATTALI, JACQUES, *Noise. The Political Economy of Music*, trans. Brian Massumi (Minneapolis: University of Minnesota Press, 1985).

AUBIGNAC, FRANÇOIS HÉDELIN, ABBÉ D', *La Pratique du théâtre* (Alger: Jules Carbonel, 1927).

—— *The Whole Art of the Stage* (1684; Bronx: Blom, 1968).

AUERBACH, ERIC, *Literary Language and its Public in Late Latin Antiquity and in the Middle Ages*, trans. Ralph Manheim (Princeton: Princeton University Press, 1965).

—— 'Figura', in *Scenes from the Drama of European Literature* (Minneapolis: University of Minnesota Press, 1984), 11–76.

BANVILLE, THÉODORE DE, *Petit Traité de versification française*, in *Œuvres*, vol. 8 (1871; Geneva: Slatkine, 1972).

BARDON, FRANÇOISE, *Le Portrait mythologique à la cour de France sous Henri IV et Louis XIII* (Paris: Picard, 1974).

BARNWELL, H. T., *The Tragic Drama of Corneille and Racine. An Old Parallel Revisited* (Oxford: Clarendon Press, 1982).

BARRAULT, JEAN-LOUIS, *Mise en scène de Phèdre* (Paris: Seuil, 1946).

BARTHES, ROLAND, *Sur Racine* (Paris: Seuil, 1963).

BASSINET, STÉPHANE (ed.), *Philippe Quinault. Atys. Edition critique* (Geneva: Droz, 1992).

BASSY, ALAIN-MARIE, 'Les Fables de La Fontaine et le Labyrinthe de Versailles', *Revue d'histoire du livre* 12 (1976), 367–424.

BAUER, LINDA FREEMAN, 'Further Reflections on an Emblematic Interpretation of Caravaggio's Early Works', *Emblematica* 7 (1993), 217–37.

—— 'Seventeenth-Century Naturalism and the Emblematic Interpretation of Paintings', *Emblematica* 3 (1988), 209–28.

BEAGLEHOLE, J. C. (ed.), *The Voyage of the Endeavour 1768–1771* (Cambridge: Cambridge University Press, 1955).

BEAUSSANT, PHILIPPE, *Lully, ou le musicien du soleil* (Paris: Gallimard, 1992).

BENJAMIN, WALTER, *Ursprung des deutschen Trauerspiels* (Frankfurt-a.-M.: Suhrkamp, 1963).

BERGER, ROBERT W., *In the Garden of the Sun King: Studies on the Park of Versailles* (Washington: Dumbarton Oaks Research Library and Collection, 1985).

—— 'Review Essay: *Manière de montrer les jardins de Versailles*', *Journal of Garden History* 4 (1984), 429–31.

BIDAR, MATHIEU, *Hippolyte* (Lille: Balthasar Le Francq, 1675).

BLANCHOT, MAURICE, *L'Espace littéraire* (Paris: Gallimard, 1955).

BLUNT, ANTHONY, The *Hypnerotomachia Poliphili* in 17th-Century France', *Journal of the Warburg Institute* 1 (1937–8), 117–37.

BOAS, GEORGE (trans.), *The Hieroglyphics of Horapollo* (Princeton: Princeton University Press, 1993).

BOILEAU-DESPRÉAUX, NICOLAS, *Dialogues, Réflexions critiques, Œuvres diverses*, ed. Charles-H. Boudhors (Paris: Belles Lettres, 1960).

—— *Epîtres, Art poétique, Lutrin*, ed. Charles-H. Boudhors (Paris: Belles Lettres, 1952).

—— *Satires, Epîtres, Art poétique* (Paris: Gallimard, 1985).

—— (trans.), *Traité du sublime, ou du merveilleux dans le discours* (Paris: Belles Lettres, 1942).

BORGEAUD, PHILIPPE, 'The Open Entrance to the Closed Palace of the King: The Greek Labyrinth in Context', *History of Religions* 14 (1974), 1–27.

BOSSUET, JACQUES BÉNIGNE, *Oraisons funèbres* (Paris: Garnier, 1961).

BOSTRÖM, HANS-OLOF, 'Philipp Hainhofer and Gustavus Adolphus's *Kunstschrank* in Uppsala', in Impey and MacGregor (eds.).

BOWIE, MALCOLM, *Lacan* (Cambridge: Harvard University Press, 1991).

BRADLEY, A. C., *Oxford Lectures on Poetry* (London: Macmillan, 1909).

BRAY, RENÉ, *La Formation de la doctrine classique en France* (Paris: Hachette, 1927).

BREMOND, HENRI, *Histoire littéraire du sentiment religieux en France depuis la fin des guerres de religion jusqu'à nos jours*, 11 vols. (1916–32; Paris: Armand Colin, 1967).

—— *La Poésie pure* (Paris: Grasset, 1926).

—— *Racine et Valéry. Notes sur l'initiation poétique* (Paris: Grasset, 1931).

BRODY, JULES, *Boileau and Longinus* (Geneva: Droz, 1958).

—— 'Pourquoi la lecture philologique?', in *Nouvelles Lectures de Montaigne* (Paris: Champion, 1994), 107–25.

BROOKS, WILLIAM, 'Seventeenth-Century Culture: Quinault and Lully Resurgent', *French Studies Bulletin* 47 (1993), 17–19.

BRUNEL, LUCIEN, *Les Philosophes et l'Académie française au dix-huitième siècle* (Paris: Hachette, 1884).

BRUNO, GIORDANO, *La Cena de le ceneri, The Ash Wednesday Supper*, trans. Edward A. Gosselin and Lawrence S. Lerner (Hamden, CT: Archon Books, 1977).

CACIOLLI, LIDIA, 'Giovanni da Falgano fra Pier Vettori e la Camerata de' Bardi', *Rinascimento* 31 (1991), 309–24.

CAHEN, JACQUES-GABRIEL, *Le Vocabulaire de Racine* (1946; Geneva: Slatkine, 1970).

CAMERARIUS, JOACHIM, *Symbolorum et emblematum ex acquatilibus et reptilibus* (1604; Graz: Akademische Druck- und Verlagsanstalt, 1988).

CERQUIGLINI, BERNARD, *Eloge de la variante. Une Histoire critique de la philologie* (Paris: Seuil, 1988).

CHARAGEAT, MARGUERITE, 'De la maison Dédalus aux labyrinthes, dans l'art des jardins, du Moyen-Age à la Renaissance', in *Actes du XVIIème congrès international d'histoire de l'art, Amsterdam 1952* (The Hague: 1955), 345–50.

CICERO, *De inventione, De optimo genere oratorum, Topica*, trans. H. M. Hubbell (London and Cambridge: William Heinemann and Harvard University Press, 1949).

CLARK, ARTHUR MELVILLE, and WHITEHALL, HAROLD, 'Rhyme', in *Princeton Encyclopedia of Poetry and Poetics*, ed. Alex Preminger (Princeton: Princeton University Press, 1974).

CLAUDEL, PAUL, *Conversation sur Jean Racine* (Paris: Gallimard, 1956).

COLLINS, WILLIAM, *The Works of William Collins*, ed. Richard Wendorf and Charles Ryskamp (Oxford: Clarendon Press, 1979).

COOMANS, HENRY E., 'Conchology Before Linnaeus', in Impey and MacGregor (eds.), 188–92.

COUTON, GEORGES, *La Poétique de La Fontaine* (Paris: PUF, 1957).

COUVREUR, MANUEL, *Jean-Baptiste Lully. Musique et dramaturgie au service du prince* (n.p.: Marc Volkar Editeur, 1992).

CRONK, NICOLAS, 'Molière-Charpentier's *Le Malade imaginaire*: the First *Opéra-comique*?', *Forum for Modern Language Studies* 29 (1993), 216–31.

—— 'The Play of Words and Music in Molière-Charpentier's *Le Malade imaginaire*', *French Studies* 47 (1993), 6–19.

DALY, PETER, *Literature in the Light of the Emblem* (Toronto: University of Toronto Press, 1985).

DE CERTEAU, MICHEL, 'Walking in the City', in *The Practice of Everyday Life*, trans. Steven R. Rendall (Berkeley, Los Angeles, London: University of California Press, 1984), 91–110.

DEJEAN, JOAN, *Ancients Against Moderns. Culture Wars and the Making of a Fin de siècle* (Chicago and London: University of Chicago Press, 1997).

DEMPSEY, CHARLES, *Annibale Carracci. The Farnese Gallery, Rome* (New York: George Braziller, 1995).

—— 'Euanthes redivivus: Rubens's *Prometheus Bound*', *Journal of the Warburg and Courtauld Institutes* 30 (1967), 420–5.

DIDEROT, DENIS, *Paradoxe sur le comédien précédé des Entretiens sur le fils naturel* (Paris: Flammarion, 1981).

DOLAR, MLADEN, 'The Object Voice', in Salecl and Žižek (eds.), 7–31.

DOOB, PENELOPE REED, *The Idea of the Labyrinth from Classical Antiquity through the Middle Ages* (Ithaca and London: Cornell University Press, 1990).

DU BELLAY, JOACHIM, *Les Regrets* [...] *suivi de La Défense et Illustration de la Langue française*, ed. S. de Sacy (Paris: Gallimard, 1967).

DU MARSAIS, CÉSAR CHESNEAU, *Des Tropes ou des différents sens* (Paris: Flammarion, 1988).

DUPONT-ROC, ROSELYNE, and LALLOT, JEAN (trans.), *Aristote. La Poétique* (Paris: Seuil, 1980).

EURIPIDES, *Hippolytus*, trans. David Grene (Chicago and London: University of Chicago Press, 1955).

FÉNELON, FRANÇOIS DE SALIGNAC DE LA MOTHE, *Lettre à l'académie* (Paris: Droz, 1970).

FITZWILLIAM MUSEUM (C[RAIG] H[ARTLEY]), *Treasures from the Fitzwilliam* (Cambridge: Cambridge University Press, 1989).

FRANCE, PETER, *Politeness and its Discontents. Problems in French Classical Culture* (Cambridge: Cambridge University Press, 1992).

FREEMAN, BRYANT C., and BATSON, ALAN, *Concordance du théâtre et des poésies de Jean Racine*, 2 vols (Ithaca: Cornell University Press, 1968).

FUMAROLI, MARC, *L'Age de l'éloquence. Rhétorique et 'res literaria' de la Renaissance au seuil de l'époque classique* (1980; Paris: Albin Michel, 1994).

FURETIÈRE, ANTOINE, *Le Dictionnaire universel* (1690; Paris: SNL-Le Robert, 1978).

GARNIER, ROBERT, *Hippolyte* (1573), in *Œuvres complètes* (Paris: Garnier, 1923), i.

GAUTIER, THÉOPHILE, *Histoire de l'art dramatique en France depuis vingt-cinq ans*, 6 vols. (Leipzig: 1858–9; Geneva: Slatkine, 1968).

GILBERT, GABRIEL, *Hypolite ou le garçon insensible* (Paris: Courbé, 1647).

GIRDLESTONE, CUTHBERT, *La Tragédie en musique (1673–1750) considérée comme genre littéraire* (Geneva: Droz, 1972).

GLÜCK, GUSTAV, and HABERDITZL, FRANZ MARTIN, *Die Handzeichnungen von Peter Paul Rubens* (Berlin: Julius Bard, 1928).

GOLD, ARTHUR, and FIZDALE, ROBERT, *The Divine Sarah. A Life of Sarah Bernhardt* (New York: Alfred Knopf, 1991).

GOLDMANN, LUCIEN, *Le Dieu caché. Etude sur la vision tragique du monde dans les Pensées de Pascal et le théâtre de Racine* (Paris: Gallimard, 1955).

GOODKIN, RICHARD E., *The Tragic Middle. Racine, Aristotle, Euripides* (Madison: University of Wisconsin Press, 1991).

GOTHEIN, MARIE LUISE, *Geschichte der Gartenkunst* (1928), 2 vols., trans. Mrs Archer-Hind (New York: Hacker Art Books, 1979).

GRAFF, GERALD, *Beyond the Culture Wars. How Teaching the Conflicts Can Revitalize American Education* (New York and London: W. W. Norton, 1992).

—— *Professing Literature: An Institutional History* (Chicago: University of Chicago Press, 1987).

GREENBLATT, STEPHEN, *Shakespearean Negotiations* (Berkeley: University of California Press, 1988).

GRISEBACH, AUGUST, *Der Garten. Eine Geschichte seiner künstlerischen Gestaltung* (Leipzig: Klinhardt & Biermann, [1910]).

GROS, ETIENNE, *Philippe Quinault. Sa vie et son œuvre* (Paris: Champion, 1926).

GRUBE, M. A. (trans.), *On Poetry and Style. Aristotle* (New York: Macmillan, 1958).

GUMBRECHT, HANS ULRICH, '"Un souffle d'Allemagne ayant passé": Friedrich Diez, Gaston Paris, and the Genesis of National Philologies', *Romance Philology* 40 (1986), 1–37.

HAN, PIERRE, 'The "Labyrinthe": A Metaphor of Dramatic Action in "Phèdre"', *South Atlantic Bulletin*, 34/4 (1969), 15–17.

HAWCROFT, MICHAEL, *Word as Action. Racine, Rhetoric, and Theatrical Language* (Oxford: Clarendon Press, 1992).

HAYMANN, EMMANUEL, *Lulli* (Paris: Flammarion, 1991).

HAZLEHURST, F. HAMILTON, *Gardens of Illusion. The Genius of André Le Nostre* (Nashville: Vanderbilt University Press, 1980).

HELD, JULIUS, *The Oil Sketches of Peter Paul Rubens* (Princeton: Princeton University Press, 1980).

HENKEL, ARTHUR, and SCHÖNE, ALBRECHT (eds.), *Emblemata. Handbuch der Sinnbildkunst des XVI. und XVII. Jahrhunderts* (Stuttgart: J. B. Metzler, 1967).

HERTZ, NIEL, 'A Reading of Longinus', in *The End of the Line. Essays on Psychoanalysis and the Sublime* (New York: Columbia University Press, 1985), 1–20.

HERZEL, ROGER W., 'Racine, Laurent, and the *Palais à volonté*', *PMLA* 108 (1993), 1064–82.

HEYER, JOHN HAJDU (ed.), *Jean-Baptiste Lully and the Music of the French Baroque. Essays in Honor of James R. Anthony* (Cambridge: Cambridge University Press, 1989).

HIRST, MICHAEL, *Michelangelo Draftsman. National Gallery, 9 October–11*

December 1988 (Milan: Olivetti, 1988).

HOMER, *The Iliad*, trans. Richard Lattimore (Chicago and London: University of Chicago Press, 1951).

HOWARTH, W. D., 'Some Thoughts on the Function of Rhyme in French Classical Tragedy', in *The Equilibrium of Wit. Essays for Odette de Mourges*, ed. Peter Bayley and Dorothy Gabe Coleman (Lexington: French Forum, 1982).

HUEBERT, MME RONALD M., 'Racine et le Labyrinthe de Versailles', *Cahiers raciniens* 28 (1970), 19–23.

IMPEY, OLIVER, and MACGREGOR, ARTHUR (eds.), *Origins of Museums: The Cabinet of Curiosities in Sixteenth- and Seventeenth-Century Europe* (Oxford: Clarendon Press, 1985).

ISHERWOOD, ROBERT M., *Music in the Service of the King: France in the Seventeenth Century* (Ithaca and London: Cornell University Press, 1973).

JAFFÉ, MICHAEL, *Rubens and Italy* (Oxford: Phaidon, 1977).

—— *Rubens. Catalogo completo* (Milan: Rizzoli, 1989).

JEHASSE, JEAN, 'De la fable aux *Fables*. Bensérade et La Fontaine', in *Mélanges offerts à Georges Couton*, ed. Jean Jehasse *et al.* (Lyon: Presses universitaires de Lyon, 1981), 323–44.

KASTNER, L. E., *A History of French Versification* (Oxford: Clarendon Press, 1903).

KERN, HERMANN, *Labirinti: Forme e interpretazioni: 5000 anni di presenza di un archetipo*, trans. Libero Sosio (Milan: Feltrinelli, 1981).

KINTZLER, CATHERINE, *Poétique de l'opéra français de Corneille à Rousseau* (Paris: Minerve, 1991).

KLIBANSKY, RAYMOND, PANOFSKY, ERWIN, and SAXL, FRITZ, *Saturn and Melancholy* (London: Nelson, 1964).

KNIGHT, R. C., *Racine et la Grèce* (Paris: Nizet, 1974).

KRETZULESCO-QUARANTA, EMANUELA, *Les Jardins du songe. 'Poliphile' et la mystique de la Renaissance*, 2nd edn. (Paris: Belles Lettres, 1986).

LACAN, JACQUES, *Le Séminaire, livre XI. Les Quatre Concepts fondamentaux de la psychanalyse* (Paris: Seuil, 1973).

LADBOROUGH, R. W., 'Translation from the Ancients in Seventeenth-Century France', *Journal of the Warburg Institute* 2 (1938), 85–104.

LA GORCE, JÉRÔME DE, and SCHNEIDER, HERBERT (eds.), *Jean-Baptiste Lully. Actes du colloque tenu à Saint-Germain-en-Laye et Heidelberg en 1987* (Laaber: Laaber-Verlag, 1990).

LA HARPE, J. F., *Cours de littérature ancienne et moderne*, 18 vols. (Paris: Dupont, 1826).

LA MOTTE, ANTOINE HOUDART DE, *Les Paradoxes littéraires ou discours écrits par cet académicien*, ed. B. Julien (1859; Geneva: Slatkine, 1971).

LANCASTER, HENRY CARRINGTON, *A History of French Dramatic Literature in the Seventeenth Century. Part IV: The Period of Racine 1673–1700*, 2 vols.

(Baltimore, Oxford and Paris: Johns Hopkins Press, Oxford University Press, Belles Lettres, 1940).
—— 'Nineteen-Forty', *PMLA* 54 (1939), 1314–24.
LANDWEHR, JOHN, *French, Italian, Spanish, and Portuguese Books of Devices and Emblems 1534–1827* (Utrecht: Haentjens Dekker & Gumbert, 1976).
LA PINELIÈRE, GUÉRIN DE, *Hippolyte* (Paris: Antoine de Sommaville, 1635).
LE CERF DE LA VIÉVILLE, JEAN LAURENT, *Comparaison de la musique italienne et de la musique françoise* (1705; Geneva: Minkoff, 1972).
LE DANTEC, DENISE, and LE DANTEC, JEAN-PIERRE, *Le Roman des jardins de France: Leur Histoire* (Paris: Plon, 1987), trans. Jessica Levine (Cambridge and London: MIT Press, 1990).
LICHTENSTEIN, JACQUELINE, *The Eloquence of Color: Rhetoric and Painting in the French Classical Age* (Berkeley: University of California Press, 1995).
LITMAN, THÉODORE A., *Le Sublime en France (1660–1714)* (Paris: Nizet, 1971).
LOUIS XIV, *Manière de montrer les jardins de Versailles* (Paris: Réunion des musées nationaux, 1992).
LOUIS, ARMEL, *Dictionnaire des rimes et assonances* (Paris: Les Usuels, 1997).
MALRAUX, ANDRÉ, *Les Voix du silence* (Paris: Gallimard, 1951).
MARIE, ALFRED, *Naissance de Versailles: Le Château, les jardins*, 2 vols. (Paris: Vincent Fréal, 1968).
MARIN, LOUIS, *Le Portrait du roi* (Paris: Minuit, 1981).
MARTIANUS CAPELLA, *De nuptiis Philologiae et Mercurii*, in *Martianus Capella and the Seven Liberal Arts*, trans. William Harris Stahl *et al.* (New York: Columbia University Press, 1922).
MAS, EMILE, *La Champmeslé* (Paris: Félix Alcan, 1932).
MASKELL, DAVID, *Racine. A Theatrical Reading* (Oxford: Clarendon Press, 1991).
MATHEWS, W. H., *Mazes and Labyrinths: Their History and Development* (1922; New York: Dover, 1970).
MAURON, CHARLES, *L'Inconscient dans la vie et l'œuvre de Jean Racine* (Aix-en-Provence: La Faculté des lettres, 1957).
MCGOWAN, MARGARET, 'Racine, Menestrier, and Sublime Effects', *Theatre Research International* 1/2 (1975), 1–13.
MENESTRIER, CLAUDE-FRANÇOIS, *Art des Emblemes* (1662; New York and London: Garland, 1979).
MESNARD, PAUL, *Histoire de l'Académie française depuis sa fondation jusqu'en 1830* (Paris: Charpentier, 1857).
—— (ed.), *Œuvres de J. Racine*, 7 vols. (Paris: Hachette, 1865–70).
MICHAELIDES, SOLON, *The Music of Ancient Greece. An Encyclopedia* (London: Faber and Faber, 1978).
MILLEN, RONALD FORSYTH, and WOLF, ROBERT ERICH, *Heroic Deeds and Mystic Figures: A New Reading of Rubens' Life of Maria de' Medici* (Princeton: Princeton University Press, 1989).

MOREAU, JEAN-BAPTISTE, *Chœurs de la tragédie d'Esther avec la music composée par J. B. Moreau, Maistre de musique du roi* (Paris: Thierry, Barbin, et Ballard, 1689).
MORIARTY, MICHAEL, *Taste and Ideology in Seventeenth-Century France* (Cambridge: Cambridge University Press, 1988).
MULLER, DOMINIQUE, 'Aspects de la déclamation dans le récitatif de Jean-Baptiste Lully', *Forum Musicologicum* 2 (1980), 231–51.
MULLER, JEFFREY M., *Rubens: The Artist as Collector* (Princeton: Princeton University Press, 1989).
MURRAY, TIMOTHY, 'The Académie Française', in *A New History of French Literature*, ed. Denis Hollier, (Cambridge and London: Harvard University Press, 1989), 267–73.
MUSSET, ALFRED DE, *Œuvres complètes* (Paris: Seuil, 1963).
NICHOLS, STEPHEN JR. (ed.), 'The New Philology', *Speculum* 65 (1990).
NIETZSCHE, FRIEDRICH, *The Complete Works of Friedrich Nietzsche*, ed. Oscar Levy (New York: Russell & Russell, 1964).
—— *Werke. Kritische Gesamtausgabe* (Berlin and New York: Walter de Gruyter, 1982).
NORA, PIERRE, 'Entre mémoire et histoire. La Problématique des lieux', in *Les Lieux de mémoire* (Paris: Gallimard, 1984), pp. xvii-xlii.
OLIVET, PIERRE-JOSEPH THOULIER ABBÉ D', *Correspondance littéraire du president Bouhier, No. 3, lettres de Pierre-Joseph Thoulier abbé d'Olivet (1719–1745)* (Université de Saint-Etienne, 1976).
—— *Remarques de grammaire sur Racine* (Paris: Gandouin, 1738).
ORLANDO, FRANCESCO, *Toward a Freudian Theory of Literature—With an Analysis of Racine's Phèdre*, trans. Charmaine Lee (Baltimore and London: Johns Hopkins University Press, 1978).
OVID, *Les Fastes*, trans. Henri Le Bonniec (Bologna: Pàtron, 1970).
—— *Metamorphoses*, trans. Mary M. Innes (Harmondsworth: Penguin, 1955).
PALISCA, CLAUDE, 'Mentor to the Florentine Camerata', *Musical Quarterly* 40 (1954), 1–20.
PARISH, RICHARD, *Racine. The Limits of Tragedy* (Paris, Seattle, Tübingen: PFSCL, 1993).
PASCAL, BLAISE, *Œuvres complètes* (Paris: Seuil, 1963).
PELLISSON FONTANIER, PAUL, and OLIVET, ABBÉ D', *Histoire de l'Académie française*, 2 vols. (Paris: Didier, 1858).
PERLOFF, MARJORIE, *Rhyme and Meaning in the Poetry of Yeats* (The Hague and Paris: Mouton, 1970).
[PERRAULT, CHARLES], *Labyrinthe de Versailles* (1677) (Paris: Moniteur, 1982).
PERRAULT, CHARLES, 'Le Labyrinthe de Versailles', in *Contes*, ed. Jean-Pierre Collinet (Paris: Gallimard, 1981), 239–57.
PERRY, BEN EDWIN (ed.), *Babrius and Phaedrus* (Cambridge: Harvard University Press, 1955).

PHILLIPS, HENRY, *Racine: Language and Theatre* (Durham: University of Durham Press, 1994).

PICARD, RAYMOND, *La Carrière de Jean Racine* (Paris: Gallimard 1956).

—— (ed.), *Racine. Œuvres complètes*, 2 vols. (Paris: Gallimard, 1952).

PIGLER, A., *Barokthemen. Eine Auswahl von Verzeichnissen zur Ikonographie des 17. und 18. Jahrhunderts* (Budapest: Verlag der ungarischen Akademie der Wissenschaften, 1956).

PIGMAN, G. W., III, 'Versions of Imitation in the Renaissance', *Renaissance Quarterly* 33 (1980), 1–23.

PILES, ROGER DE, *Conversations sur la connoissance de la peinture, et sur le jugement qu'on doit faire des tableaux* (Paris: Nicolas Langlois, 1677).

PRADON, JACQUES, *Phèdre et Hippolyte*, ed. O. Classe (Exeter: University of Exeter, 1987).

PROUST, MARCEL, *Albertine disparue* (Paris: Gallimard, 1989).

—— *Correspondance*, ed. Philip Kolb (Paris: Plon, 1984).

PUTTFARKEN, THOMAS, *Roger de Piles' Theory of Art* (New Haven and London: Yale University Press, 1985).

QUINTILLIAN, *Institutio oratoria*, 4 vols., trans. H. E. Butler (London: Heinemann, 1920–2).

RACINE, JEAN, *Œuvres complètes* (Paris: Seuil, 1962).

RACINE, LOUIS, 'Mémoires sur la vie et les ouvrages de Jean Racine', in *Racine. Œuvres complètes*, ed. Raymond Picard (Paris: Gallimard, 1952).

—— *Remarques sur les tragédies de Jean Racine* (1752), in *Œuvres complètes*, 6 vols. (1808; Geneva: Slatkine, 1969).

RAVAISSON, FRANÇOIS, *Archives de la Bastille*, 16 vols. (Paris: A. Durand et Pedone-Lauriel, 1866–83).

ROHOU, JEAN, *Jean Racine: entre sa carrière, son œuvre, et son Dieu* (Paris: Fayard, 1992).

RUSSELL, DANIEL, *The Emblem and Device in France* (Lexington: French Forum, 1985).

—— *Emblematic Structures in Renaissance French Culture* (Toronto: University of Toronto Press, 1995).

SALECL, RENATA, and ŽIŽEK, SLAVOJ (eds.), *Gaze and Voice as Love Objects* (Durham and London: Duke University Press, 1996).

SANTARCHANGELI, PAOLO, *Le Livre des labyrinthes: Histoire d'un mythe et d'un symbole*, trans. Monique Lacau (Paris: Gallimard, 1974).

SCARRON, PAUL, *Poésies diverses*, ed. Maurice Cauchie, 2 vols (Paris: Didier, 1947).

SCHEURLEER, TH. H., 'Early Dutch Cabinets of Curiosities', in Impey and MacGregor (eds.), 115–20.

SCHILLER, FREDERICK (trans.), *Phädra* (1805; Stuttgart: Reclam, 1955).

SCOTT, CLIVE, *French Verse-art: A Study* (Cambridge: Cambridge University Press, 1980).

—— *The Riches of Rhyme* (Oxford: Clarendon Press, 1988).

SCUDÉRY, MADELEINE DE, *Promenade de Versailles* (1669; Geneva: Slatkine, 1979).

SEGAL, CHARLES, *Language and Desire in Seneca's Phaedra* (Princeton: Princeton University Press, 1986).

SEILERN, ANTOINE, *Catalogue of Paintings and Drawings at 56 Princes Gate, London* (London: Shenval Press, 1955–71).

SENECA, LUCIUS ANNAEUS, *Phaedra*, in *Seneca. Three Tragedies*, trans. Frederick Ahl (Ithaca and London: Cornell University Press, 1986).

—— *Phaedra*, in *Seneca's Tragedies*, trans. Frank Justus Miller (Cambridge: Harvard University Press, 1953).

SONINO, ANNALISE SCARPA, *Cabinet d'amateur. Le Grandi Collezioni d'arte nei dipinti dal XVII al XIX secolo* (Milan: Berenice, 1992).

SORIANO, MARC, *Le Dossier Charles Perrault* (Paris: Hachette, 1972).

SPITZER, LEO, 'The "Récit de Théramène"', in *Linguistics and Literary History. Essays in Stylistics* (1948; New York: Russell & Russell, 1962).

STAROBINSKI, JEAN, 'Racine et la poétique du regard', in *L'Œil vivant* (Paris: Gallimard, 1961), 69–90.

STELAND, DIETER, 'Racines *Phèdre* in den Übersetzungen von Friedrich Schiller und Simon Werle', *Zeitschrift für französische Sprache und Literatur* 102 (1992), 64–78.

STENDHAL, *Racine et Shakespeare* (1823, 1825; Geneva: Slatkine, 1986).

STRACHEY, LYTTON, 'Racine' (1908), in *Books and Characters French & English* (New York: Harcourt, Brace, 1922).

STRAVINSKY, IGOR, and CRAFT, ROBERT, *Dialogues* (Berkeley: University of California Press, 1982).

SUBLIGNY, ADRIEN THOMAS PERDOU DE, *Dissertation sur les tragédies de Phèdre et d'Hippolyte* (Paris: Sercy, 1677).

TEYSSÈDRE, BERNARD, *Roger de Piles et les débats sur le coloris au siècle de Louis XIV* (Paris: Bibliothèque des arts, 1957).

TRUC, GONZAGUE, *Jean Racine: l'œuvre, l'artiste, l'homme et le temps* (Paris: Garnier, 1926).

—— 'La "Nouveauté" dans la langue de Racine', *Revue d'histoire littéraire de la France* 22 (1915), 132–46.

VALÉRY, PAUL, 'Discours sur Henri Bremond', in *Œuvres*, 2 vols. (Paris: Gallimard, 1957), i. 763–9.

[VALLADIER, A.], *Le Labyrinthe royal de l'Hercule gaulois triomphant* (Avignon: Jaques Bramereau, 1601).

VAN DE PASSE, CRISPIN, *Metamorphoseon Ovidianarum* (Cologne: 1602).

VAUGELAS, CLAUDE FAVRE DE, *Remarques sur la langue françoise*, ed. Jeanne Streicher (Paris: Droz, 1934).

VETTORI, PIER, *Comentarii in primum librum Aristotles De arte poetarum*, 2nd edn. (Florence: In Officina Juntarum, Bernardi Filiorum, 1573).

VIALA, ALAIN, *Racine. La Stratégie du caméléon* (Paris: Seghers, 1990).

VIDAL-NAQUET, PIERRE, *Le Chasseur noir. Formes de pensées et formes de société dans le monde grec* (Paris: Maspero, 1983).

VINAVER, EUGÈNE (ed.), *Racine. Principes de la tragédie en marge de la Poétique d'Aristote* (Manchester and Paris: Manchester University Press and Nizet, 1978).

VIRGIL, *The Aeneid*, trans. W. F. Jackson Knight (Harmondsworth: Penguin, 1956).

VOLTAIRE, *Correspondance*, ed. Theodore Besterman (Geneva: Institut et musée Voltaire, 1959).

—— *La Henriade*, ed. O. R. Taylor, in *The Complete Works of Voltaire* (Geneva: Institut et musée Voltaire, 1970), ii.

—— 'Préface de l'édition [d'*Œdipe*] de 1730', *Œuvres complètes de Voltaire*, nouvelle édition, *Théâtre*, vol. 1 (Paris: Garnier, 1877).

WEBER, WILLIAM, 'Beyond Zeitgeist: Recent Work in Music History', *Journal of Modern History* 66 (1994), 321–45.

WEINBERG, KURT, 'The Lady and the Unicorn, or M. De Nemours à Coulommiers: Enigma, Device, Blazon and Emblem in *La Princesse de Clèves*', *Euphorion* 71 (1977), 306–35.

WHITNEY, WILLIAM DWIGHT (ed.), *The Century Dictionary and Cyclopedia, with a New Atlas of the World. A Work of General Reference in all Departments of Knowledge* (New York: The Century Company, 1889–91).

WILHELM, JACQUES, 'Le Labyrinthe de Versailles', *Revue de l'histoire de Versailles et de Seine-et-Oise* 38 (1936), 44–63.

WILKINSON, JAMES, 'A Choice of Fictions: Historians, Memory, Evidence', *PMLA* 111 (1996), 80–92.

WOODBRIDGE, KENNETH, *Princely Gardens: The Origins and Development of the French Formal Style* (London: Thames & Hudson, 1986).

WYGANT, AMY, 'Boileau and the Sound of Satire', *Forum for Modern Language Studies* 31 (1995), 128–39.

—— 'Corneille, Rubens, and the Heroic Emblem', *Emblematica*, 9 (1995), 111–32.

—— 'Leo Spitzer's Racine', *MLN* 109 (1994), 632–49.

—— 'Medea, Poison, and the Epistemology of Error in *Phèdre*', *MLR*, forthcoming, 1999.

YATES, FRANCES, *The Art of Memory* (London: Routledge, 1966).

ZUBER, ROGER, *Les 'Belles Infidèles' et la formation du goût classique. Perrot d'Ablancourt et Guez de Balzac* (Paris: Armand Colin, 1968).

INDEX

9781900755146